SEANA MARENA

Journey through Africa

PATRICK BYERS

Bloomington, IN Milton Keynes, UK

authorHOUSE

AuthorHouse™
1663 Liberty Drive, Suite 200
Bloomington, IN 47403
www.authorhouse.com
Phone: 1-800-839-8640

AuthorHouse™ UK Ltd.
500 Avebury Boulevard
Central Milton Keynes, MK9 2BE
www.authorhouse.co.uk
Phone: 08001974150

This book is a work of non-fiction. Unless otherwise noted, the author and the publisher make no explicit guarantees as to the accuracy of the information contained in this book and in some cases, names of people and places have been altered to protect their privacy.

First published by AuthorHouse 11/1/2006

ISBN: 1-4259-4211-3 (sc)
ISBN: 1-4259-5256-9 (dj)

Library of Congress Control Number: 2006904925

Printed in the United States of America
Bloomington, Indiana

This book is printed on acid-free paper.

INTRODUCTION

New York City, April 3, 2004. A question. What does Felix Mendelssohn's *Trio in D minor* have in common with the Amazon river, Ho Chi Minh City, Vietnam, and the Lakota peoples of North Dakota? This story will answer the question. To you, the reader, it will be evident that one journey created a need for another. The odd concoction will be rare to you. It is truthful, perhaps romanticized, a weakness many westerners have recounting an experience in Africa.

I am a composer of symphonies, sonatas, and operas. Vienna, Paris, London, New York City are the capitols of music making for my skills. A composer's work traditionally lists recordings, concerts, reviews, and awards. A press interview includes the reasons for the music's inspiration made spicy by accounts of various muses in an artist's life.

Back in the winter of 1986 I did fall in love. This muse made a fool out of me. Even so, I burned the western-destiny bridge. I have never looked back.

I believe there is a Mozart growing up in the township of Soweto, South Africa. A Mozart with black skin whose life will create a startling presence in classical music. Through this individual the world will return to Africa where we originated. We will dance and we will sing. Harsh downbeats will become history. The sunny joy from the violent African soil will reawaken the west from the slumber we live with, cutting out noise, a noise we have proudly recorded as our history.

Another question: Why a Mozart in South Africa? Mozart composed his operas in his native language while others in his country composed in Italian. He was a prankster, a bit of a trouble maker for the status quo. He bathed the west with music and made for the western culture a standard so high that the west has dubbed his influence 'the Mozart effect'. Like an eager child I want to tell my story in order to get to its heart. It began when apartheid held the black man in chains, an unlikely place for the human heart. I had chosen the life of a composer. I had no idea that the love of creating music would place a death grip on my life. I fell hopelessly in love with South Africa, February of 1986. Everywhere there was war. Fear of catastrophic bloodshed was in every conversation. A black ruled South Africa was to many a dream, equally to many a harbinger of decay. In the midst of this Napoleonic struggle, a music that belonged first to Africa inspired every heart that beat in this tragedy no matter what was hoped or feared.

I was a friend. I saw a role for music and expressed it. Military transport planes flew overhead, bombs went off in the middle of the night. What was the usual daily life to most, was terrifying for me. I returned again many times finding those who could lead me. Close to nervous collapse, isolated from lack of comprehension in the west, accused at one point of being an enemy of the government, I did find what I sought.

I was trusted eventually by peoples in conflict. I consider this a gift. I have waited to tell my story as a measure of trust. Six months before Mr. Mandela was released from prison to a stunned world, I was told in confidence that this was to happen. I did not betray trust for personal gain.

I insisted South Africa could survive under black rule, simply because South Africa was driven by economic infrastructure, not agrarian, as was the case in Zimbabwe. The gold and diamonds which built one of the great performance theaters in the world in Pretoria could guarantee that majority rule in time could bring South Africa into first world infrastructure.

I know through a friend that my words went to Mr. DeKlerk. Much was already under way at that point, so I do not presume to be that catalyst. I do know I was trusted, and in fact, loved as a true friend of South Africa in the darkest hours.

On my final return trip to New York, standing among 300 passengers to board, I was stopped at the gate. The South African Airways official studied the passenger list on the computer. He asked me to wait. A supervisor was called to the boarding gate, and he looked at the computer, then he looked at me. He informed me that my seat assignment had been upgraded. He offered no explanation, but I knew. It was a thank you from the quiet people who were soon to yield power without war and bloodshed. The world celebrated, the noisy western world, to which I returned, a world that had no clue as to why this happened. I knew.

You see it had to do with Felix Mendelssohn, Mozart, oh yes, and Gustav Mahler's *Resurrection Symphony*, and the remarkable people on both sides of the conflict who extended trust to a composer of symphonies.

In the years since then, my music has returned to recordings, performances, and a growing respect. My children's voices noisily bounce off the walls of my apartment accompanying a sonata. The students at the *Fame* high school dance to my music and treat me like a rock star. Other music-searching journeys were made simply because they 'felt' like South Africa. Living has continued and *life is long*. I learned this from a man in South Africa.

Walking in my neighborhood, Harlem, I often hear an accent I recognize as African. On the subway I've heard the familiar Afrikaner rhythms of speech. The South African English I hear every day from a colleague at school who is from Durban. I have Beryl Markam's *West with the Night* safely in my library alongside Alan Paton, Nadine Gordimer, and copies of two films created from my days in South Africa. I have memories from an experience rich with drama, love, fear, death, and redemption.

The musicians I met at the end of my journey have become the cultural music ambassadors for their new country. Heeding my counsel, they shifted their music towards Africa. Here, I was the catalyst, the one who saw and spoke. You will not see my name in their story. That is as is should be. Their courage to alter their classical training towards the rhythms of their birth heritage entitles them to ownership. They will smile if you ask them about me. We became friends during dark days. I own those hours. They belong to my destiny-burnt western bridge.

It will take the usual book reading hours to absorb the basic thrift of this journey. You will, reader, I hope, be a bit altered at its conclusion, if perhaps later in your life should you decide to become a fool from a consuming passion.

Such a decision can be made by anyone.

PART ONE

CHAPTER 1
Francois Odendaal

The Amazon, August 1985. Francois Odendaal was a zoologist. When I met him in the fall of 1985, he was researching the mating cycles of butterflies. In the lab at Duke University he survived on research grants in order to keep his position, often surviving on a wing and a prayer. When he first arrived at Duke University he had to wait a month for his first paycheck. In order to quell hunger he visited fast food places eating food left on the tables. Francois worked on his doctoral thesis in Australia living in the outback. Had not friendly farmers offered an occasional meal, he would have starved. From those days he had with him a wild dingo, his constant companion. Derry accompanied Francois on an expedition down the Colville River in Alaska, a film called *Dingo in Alaska*, the result of Derry's trip down the river with Francois. Only Francois could handle or talk with Derry. I was warned, and a careless greeting from me showed Derry's sharp, glaring teeth. Francois found him as a puppy whose mother most likely had been shot by farmers in the outback of Australia. The inside of Francois' car dangled with upholstery the result of Derry being left in the car while Francois did an errand. At an elementary school where Derry was the star after a film viewing of *Dingo in Alaska*, the mutilated car was a point of confusion to the students who could not figure out why such a famous man drove a trashed jalopy.

I was asked to create a new film score for *Dingo in Alaska* which coincided with a new English version of the film. Originally edited in Afrikanse, Francois wanted to sell it to American distributors.

Francois Odendaal, an Afrikaner, was charming. He rolled his "r's", had stories of world adventures, and lived on the edge. He led a charmed life. Surviving polio as a child in Africa, his father a doctor, his mother a devoted fan, Francois escaped death regularly. Getting caught in a whirlpool on a river in South Africa, he and a friend were sucked into a maelstrom. Francois lost consciousness, then awakened on the river bank his teeth clenched to a tree root. It was a painful memory. His friend was never found. Francois related a story unique to African lore. He did so as a skeptic true to a scientist. Yet as an African, some non western way of seeing life resonated within him telling the story. A seer in a meeting near his home had been 'contacted' by Francois' friend to let him know that a crocodile waiting at the bottom of the whirlpool had killed him. The friend wanted , according to the seer, for Francois to know all was well and for Francois to have peace of mind.

The dual poles in Francois' nature, one western trained, the other African born, resulted in a complex and fascinating human being.

Francois' major goal in his life centered around the Amazon River. Before I met him he had already traveled a major artery of the Amazon from its source in the mountains. Again a close call nearly took his life. On that expedition, he climbed the mountain leading to the artery, and contracted high altitude sickness. The crisis was grave. He was too sick to turn back as the return journey was too long. The only choice was to continue farther up the mountain, the shorter route, crossing it, and descend to the other side before his body's system collapsed. He survived.

Undaunted, he planned the next expedition, the Apurimac, in Peru. This source high in the mountains led to deadly waters, and a stretch through the Acabomba Abyss. No one before Francois had survived this monster whose canyon walls prevented any rescue once entered. The goal was to kyak from source to sea in Brazil and document the attempt with a film.

When we met, he had organized a group of people from five nations to make the attempt with him. One of these was Jack Jourgensen, who invested his money in the expedition. Jack lived in Wyoming. He had made a small fortune with household paints. Jack, to me, favored Ernest Hemingway, both with his physical swagger, pipe smoking, and need for rough adventures.

The reader should know that several books on this expedition are in print. Joe Kane's, *Running the Amazon* achieved national attention garnishing praise for its hair-raising account of this eccentric trip. Francois Odendaal published *Rafting the Amazon* in Great Britain, equally critically praised. A film, *Amazon* aired on the Discovery Channel. The film is where my story begins.

August, 1985, preparing for the journey, Jack and Francois invited me to join them as composer for the film yet to be made. Originally, they would bring me down once they were on the calmer waters of the Amazon in Brazil in order for me to collect music from the region. I agreed. Heartily.

November of 1985, I learned that Jack Jourgensen had pulled out. He had nearly drowned in one of the violent sections of the river in Peru. Unique to this group's downright luck, they had successfully navigated the Acabomba Abyss. Francois as a scientist had mapped the canyon. The Royal Geographic Society in London invited him to present his chartered maps to them. He was made a member because of the accomplishment. With Jack he went to London, temporarily leaving the river to meet with the society. During his absence, mutinous arguments erupted as to Francois' competence to lead. When Francois returned to the Amazon war broke out in the ranks, sides formed, and Francois was left with two fronts, the river and his crew. A touchy meeting with Peru's *Shining Path*, a guerilla organization in Peruvian jungles, split the group into divisions that compromised the expedition's safety. Francois' fluent Spanish and his politically leftist past quieted the guerillas distrust, and they were allowed to proceed. Francois told me that back in South Africa he had been pulled aside by Afrikaner Bruderbond and cautioned his leftist political tendencies were not appropriate for the Afrikaner people. Francois' friendships with the native peoples in Southwest Africa (Namibia) created a bond that made him wary of the prevalent Afrikaner line at that time.

Kayaking was classified as an international athletic sport under sanctions. Leftist as Francois' politics were , it did not help the athletic boycott in place against South Africa at the Brazilian border. None of the South African's were allowed to enter. The film *Amazon* ended with Francois standing alone on a Peruvian side of the Amazon waving to the remainder of the crew who would arrive at the mouth of the Amazon February, 1986. It was painful to look at his face in the film. I saw this image often while scoring and editing the music for its finish and preparation for broadcast.

Their adventure was over. Mine was to begin. I never saw the Amazon in Brazil. I saw it in South Africa through a film that I composed the music for, carried away by a composer's romanticism, rapids of its own mighty river, a romanticism gleaned from the charm of an Afrikaner dreamer. When it was my turn, I stood, my knees wobbled, my mind spun out of control , as unbalanced as a wildly spiraling nightmare. I inhaled a deep breath of fool's air and stepped out into the internal wilderness whose boundaries are western safety. It was exhilarating and at the same time terrifying.

My adventure would prove to be everything I feared and dreamt.

Somewhere in the first weeks of January, 1986, Francois made arrangements for me to take my score to South Africa. I applied for a visa. I was to travel first to Kansas City to create a score to *Othello* for Missouri Rep. I would wait to hear from Francois that week. Jack Jourgensen had decided to go with me to South Africa. There were still rumblings from the mutiny on the river, and allegiances shifted by the hour. Francois was fighting for the film's life. If he won I would go.

I had a score for *Dingo in Alaska* and *Amazon*. Usually film is cut then music added. Due to the nature of this divided story, it was decided the documentary would be cut to my music. I had great musicians playing the score. Dan Ashe, french horn, had recorded in Hollywood. One of Barbra Streisand's albums had his horn solos. John Ellis, oboe and english horn, had recorded for television and in Spielberg's *Close Encounters of the Third Kind,* he recorded the oboe tracks for the meeting with the aliens, when John William's signature tune was battered around with tuba and oboe. Thus, these two scores were made for films based on a collection of river rats risking their lives for glory. These film scores had world class musicians.

During my hours waiting to find out whether I was going to South Africa I listened to these scores and lived in reverie the possible adventure. First, I had to compose music for *Othello* that centered around a black man's passion for a white woman and his tragic blind jealousy. Even Shakespeare was waiting to go to South Africa.

Peter Bennett was glad to see me. Directing the production of Missouri Rep's *Othello,* Peter had insisted the theater contract me to compose the score for the theatre. He lived in New York, and for many plays used my particular approach to music for plays. He was insightful and easy to gain inspiration for unique ways of using music in a play. I remained in his graces for years. Eventually we created an opera that premiered in New York City at the *Theater for the New City*. Like Icarus our chariot aimed very high, and out of sync, he disassociated his work from mine. It was a tragic loss March of 2001.

February of 1986 we were excited about the challenge of that production of *Othello.* Peter went out of his way to make a comfortable position for me among the other production heads. As an introduction to the theater arrangements were made for me to see the play that was running. It was a Sunday afternoon matinee.

When I arrived and took my seat I read the program. *Master Harold and the Boys,* by Athol Fugard. As I watched the play listening to American actors' feigned South African accent, a voice stirred inside, "wake up....", and the beginning of my adventure answered, "begin...here".

Phantoms, boyhood friendships, carefree days built from impractical dreaming drew my habit-guarded thoughts towards the real society Athol Fugard presented that Sunday afternoon. In Kansas City, Missouri, South Africa was on the horizon. Fugard mapped the pain of human bondage living in a society structured on the separation of the races.

Each day following the play I waited to hear. By the week's end as Peter Bennett and I were finishing our work, I had heard nothing.

I confessed to Peter my anxiety and eagerness to know I was going. He had a way of raising his eye brows that communicated concern. It was a very dangerous place to go. I appeared immune to anyone's note of caution. Peter knew that. He also knew I had a wild wind to follow, and it made the music he loved from me, and, thus, he never questioned the reckless side. In this confidence he was certain I would soon leave for South Africa.

That Sunday I went to bed resigning to silence. 6:30 am Monday a phone call from Francois informed me I was to go. I had to be at Kennedy that day for a flight at 7:30 pm. In a hurry I packed with the assistance of one of the actors, who cut my hair while I was in motion, drove me to a bank, then the airport. I was suffering overnight with a toothache which remained throughout the day.

I was going. In the frantic rush of the morning, Francois' hastily conveyed words sparked multicolored images of South Africa. Now, wide awake I was transported to the imagination's runway, peoples with strange customs, rare languages, a war raging, and most of all, a world of new music. I felt cleansed.

6000 miles away South Africa was a paradise for white people, an inferno for the black people. Because of sanctions talented youth were isolated. I would come to know a nation of dreamers.

"Enjoy my beautiful country," Francois had said over the phone that morning.

At the trailer in the countryside outside Duke University where Francois lived with Derry, I learned that as a teenager Francois played the bassoon and had considered a career as a musician until he one summer carved a log into a canoe and took off down the Limpopo river switching his interest to zoology. He then related to me a strange dream he had had which included me. In the dream we were both conducting an orchestra in performance. I was center stage, he was on the side standing on stairs conducting another group. Feeling vulnerable, he would look at me as he strategically determined what beat to give to his musicians. I believe the African in Francois was his orchestra while I had the western musicians, and true to dominance of the west, that part of him depended on getting cues.

While with him at his isolated trailer in the boonies our fates crossed. There was something about the early morning sun, particularly as we stood under the tall one hundred year old trees that brought back memories of summer camps and picnic dinners, where grandparents had a place of honor competing for the title of the best made fried chicken, potato salad, corn casserole, or pecan pie. It was potent. It has remained an image in me firm, untarnished, and comforting. As Francois walked with me and I enjoyed my country's birthright, he seemed, in contrast, to be feeling troubled. He had a far away, distant look in his eyes. His country was burning.

Between the two of us a slumbering giant awakened in me. Eyes opened , a fire burned while the sleepy breezes blew away the morning's dawn.

On the 3rd of March, 1986, at 7.30 pm I boarded a South African plane at Kennedy International Airport with Jack Jourgensen and left New York City for South Africa. I had a terrible toothache.

CHAPTER 2
Far away places

The 747 wide-bodied South African Airways plane flew through rough headwinds, the plane more like a ship rolling on large waves of sea air. On the plane, English and Afrikanse were the languages instructing passengers, first in English followed by Afrikanse. Afrikanse rolled the "r's" with guttural "g's". Listening as a musician to this exotic language ignited a boyhood memory 30,000 feet above the Atlantic ocean.

Deplaning at Isle de Sal off the northwest coast of Africa, Jack Jourgensen and I entered a terminal. Portuguese waiters managed a run down bar with slow moving overhead fans. Waiting to refuel the plane in this exotic hole in the wall, I returned to the boyhood memory.

I felt like a virgin traveler to far away places. *Far away places,* it was a popular song back in 1964 when I was 14 and had a friend with the uncommon name, Ishmael Jackson West. He lived in Higgston, Georgia. As colorful as his name, Jack was lanky with a boyish, impy face and a part in his two front teeth. He loved actor Terry Thomas, who had the same space in his front teeth. I had boring straight teeth. Jack claimed mastery on the subject of Ho Chi Minh. This included an original piano piece composed by him played on the black keys. He boasted he had life fully planned. Once in manhood, he intended to marry a very large woman. With 14 children, the wife and children would run the farm. He would sit on the front porch overseeing farm life while playing his tuba "in the evening". In rural Georgia this was from 2:00 pm on.

We met at a park in Dublin, Georgia. Tall pine dotted a central community park area with a creek running through the center. The park ended near a one story public high school surrounded by homes with porch swings.

Jack came along at an opportune time. He became my only friend in this isolated deep South town where 14 year old boys with flight of the imagination were considered odd. For us social life was non existent. I could not afford the penny loafer shoes, stiff collared pressed shirts or the sexy thin belts that opened doors to Georgia belles with their soft beguiling sensual accents.

Jack had magic, at least over me. Both of us entered girl-crazy years not good at soothing the madness. We lived it out in fantasy. There we were brilliant and always a success with romance. He could spin a tale like other great southern story tellers. A romance extemporaneously created by Jack West left me staring off into space. Once there, he would knock me to the ground laughing at me pleased his narrative had succeeded. I remained his victim for two years. It ended when I went "north" to study concert piano.

Every morning during my visits to Higgston, Georgia, we helped Jack's father at his country store. There were wood floors with small isles and shelves filled with a plethora of goods. The store had a sweet smell from fresh bread daily delivered. Farmer locals gathered socially in front sitting on wood crates. When the wives and daughters came to shop and rope their husbands home, I wondered which young country girl would gain in girth enough to become Jack's wife and farm manager, going into labor at least 14 times for him.

Finished with our duties we returned to Jack's house where we listened to music. He had a 33 rpm recording of orchestral arrangements of popular songs. There were sounds of sea gulls and ocean surf for Ebb Tide and Far Away Places mixed with glossy strings. We didn't talk while the records played. He lived in his imagination on his farm sitting on the front porch. His eyes closed, his mouth looked like he was playing the tuba. I was off to see the world eyes wide open.

Those hot, summer dog-days we often walked on the railroad tracks like Huck Finn and Tom Sawyer, on our way to see a "picher" show in Vidalia, Georgia where we were hopeful some beautiful country girl would share an RC Cola with us. Jack's friendship secured the flight of my imagination.

I still journey to far away places remembering Jack West and Higgston, Georgia. When we returned to the plane, I discovered it would be another 10 hours to Johannesburg. My toothache increased each hour replacing a boyhood memory with painful reality.

My imagination returned in full bloom when the 747 South African Airways jet landed at Jan Smuts International 19 hours after leaving JFK. Summer months and warm breezes greeted me contrasting the winter we had left in New York City. Jet lag and my toothache turned me inside out. Thought and reflection ceased. I began experiencing in a new way. I was unguarded, openly commenting on what was around me. Jack Jourgensen was also more talkative than usual. A man used to power arriving in South Africa, he carried the glory of American business enterprise. In contrast, I was a doddering fool.

"You're a romantic, I'm a realist," he remarked to me.

"You ignore reality. Every minute must be a fantastic tale. You are, consequently, self-important. Your views betray someone who must live every dull moment for some justification, purpose, or grand design," he assessed.

A rich man's reality. A composer's dreams.

Jack Jourgensen arrived in South Africa having no dream, only a lust for dangerous adventures, a privilege his wealthy American status promised him. By the time he returned to the US, the vitality of romanticism rubbed off on him. I would, on the other hand, feel the full blows of reality.

Jack's business acumen overwhelmed Philip Hattingh, film editor, and Pierre Van Heerden, cameraman. Meeting us, they drove us to the Burgerspark Hotel in Pretoria. Jack checked into an adjoining room to mine.

Alone, unpacking bags, reality settled. I was in South Africa. It was evening. I had not seen what South Africa looked like in daylight. I imagined dizzying photographs of the African bush violent and full of drama. Opening my window, I saw varieties of new plants and flowers, the scents new, fresh. It was my first impression, and true to first impressions, has lasted. It will remain to me Africa.

A bell hop brought some amenities. After I tipped him, he bowed and said, "thank you, boss". His gentle manner and humble demeanor touched me. He exuded graceful civility.

His gesture might have passed as insignificant except that as the days in South Africa progressed, the moment with the bell hop became a seed. Planted in the soil of dreaming, it grew into a theme. It would sing a song in the hearts of the South African people and I would hear again and again their dream from which a reality continued to hold fulfillment out of reach, a dream made to feel unreal by those who were privileged in South Africa.

At breakfast the following morning, I could see Pretoria in daylight. Sitting under umbrella shaded tables, eating fresh fruits, drinking coffee, and smoking a cigarette casually, I saw an ordered, clean first world city. This was not a poor African city. There were a lot of people doing very well. Among the hotel guests there were tables of black businessmen. The wait staff served to distraction responding to the impatient commands of a barking manager.

When Jack Jourgensen joined me for breakfast he had much to say about the overt prejudices he had heard from Philip Hattingh and Pierre Van Heerden the preceding evening. These men considered themselves progressive, and Jack was , for Jack, stunned at the isolation evident in their explanations and defense of South African good life. With the cheap labor from the South African black, both men had gardeners, house maids, nannies, and film crew. The justification came from giving jobs to people who would starve without work. Laborers traveled from the townships to their homes begging for small jobs to do for paltry sums. Minimum wage did not exist in South Africa in 1986.

After breakfast conversation, I, having kept quiet, knew one fact. I was in love with South Africa. I think about this often. I believe that my passion grew from being in love with a nightmare. South Africa was Oz. Oz darkened by invasion. South Africa with isolation, natural and human violence, mixed with the breezes of African summer. South Africa welcomed me, a lost son of her dreamers, having been born instead in a "realist's" continent.

It was a new day. My passion would grow in time becoming full. Fear vanished. Work on *Amazon and Dingo in Alaska* would soon begin. The days and night's smaller hours would blend the African day with her cooler nights. I would no longer be a hardened prisoner of life. I would not see the tragic blemishes for two years. Even when I did, I would carry the pain of love not hate for South Africa. Until my days in South Africa I understood love in warm, fuzzy terms. Soon I would discover a side to love that included violent rage, anger at injustice that unlike what I first misunderstood those first days at the Burgerspark Hotel, finds warm and fuzzy feelings cheap. In fact, there is a love that with fire yearns for forgiveness and righteousness.

Later that day, alone, I experienced convulsions. Weeping, something in me altered dramatically.

I was in a country I would love the rest of my confused life on earth.

CHAPTER 3
Waiting and Watching

Philip Hattingh edited the rushes of what would become *Amazon*. Jack Jourgensen brought with us two large boxes of film shot up to the point Francois was denied entrance into Brazil.

The artistic decisions made early came from a meeting that included my contributions. An ancient Inca ruins, Machu Picchu, had a legend of a river goddess who warned travelers on the river. This was an unconventional theme for a documentary. A goddess who warned men rang a "for whom the bell tolls" empathy with Francois' African side, my romanticism, and Jack's lust for adventure.

Jack claimed to have heard a voice off the canyon walls a short while before his close call with death. At the meeting discussing the theme for the documentary, he pulled a stone from his pocket that had come from the river bottom where the whirlpool trapped him until an oar from one of the experienced kayakers braving the deadly water reached Jack and pulled him free.

Once the film rushes were processed for editing, Jack and Philip looked at the eight hours of raw material. Documentary film told a story from what was shot. It was crucial to have critical takes on film. A crew on documentaries cannot ask a drowning man in the Amazon river to "take two".

Viewing the rushes of intense sections of the expedition Jack and Philip discovered that because of a small slither of film stuck in the camera lens, many cans of film were useless.

The river goddess became the star and theme as a result of this debacle. Otherwise, there were only groups of people discussing the dangers of what they were soon to deal with and nothing else. Francois' fate ending his dream to Kyak the mighty Amazon from source to sea was to be thwarted by his not heeding the warnings of the river goddess. Joe Kane and the others who arrived at the sea became modern man's triumph over superstition.

I am the river, the river goddess warned, I will always be the river. If you understand...come. The film would open and close with this mantra. It would turn a traditional documentary into an art film. The choice was to return to the Amazon river and re-shoot. This was impossible. My score leant itself to editing with a river goddess since I had included a Peruvian samponia, a quena, Francois playing an Australian didjereedo, and some tiny ocarinas mixed to sound as though they came out of the river's echo off canyon walls. I had contracted an African flute specialist from the *Chuck Davis Dance* troupe who mastered the samponia for the recording session. This particular instrument Francois had brought with him from Peru. During the recording session it fell apart many times since the pipes were tied together with string. It was a pan-flute in structure and had to be carefully held as the player placed his embouchure over each pipe to get a musical ambience.

The editing of *Amazon,* an art film centered around a lust for adventure. It now belonged to Philip Hattingh, film editor, and me, composer. Philip enjoyed the challenge. He edited with rhythm and became familiar with my score, assuring Jack the final edit would establish a new format for documentary film.

The copy or narration for the film was to be created towards the end. Jack took this part happily. His Ernest Hemingway likeness gained footing with pages of narration edited on the spur of the moment while Philip cut and I listened.

There were many days Philip worked alone without Jack or me. Word spread among film makers Jack Jourgensen was in South Africa with a film for the American market resulting in interest from these film makers frozen by sanctions. He often went to Johannesburg.

Left to my own wanderings, feeling confused and energized by South Africa, I wanted other experiences apart from the male braggadocio dominating the making of Amazon. I would not have to go farther than outside the editing room. We met to edit Amazon at Teknikon in Pretoria. Since it was summer, the door to the editing room was left open. Each morning students would pass by the editing room glancing in to take a peek at the Americans. Word had spread in the school that we were there and we became the American section of the Pretoria zoo. For a while, I was careful and reserved, only nodding a greeting. Jack commented on the unusual beauty of South African girls, and Philip warned me that making love to any of these under 25 could result in a jail term, particularly for Americans. This improvised piece of nonsense spread to other South African peers of Philip's. They waited to bait me should I give them the opportunity.

Soon after Philip Hattingh's set up, I gave his collection of buddies their opportunity. I did not do so accepting the challenge. I was in a stupor from a muse apart from my role in Amazon. The river goddess warned me from Machu Picchu, I am the river. *I will always be the river...if you understand...come.*

My life threatening rapids were created by men from the apartheid ruled South Africa. The warnings off the canyon walls of the Amazon river heard by Jack Jourgensen, came from real voices in days to come. The river goddess created from myth in the evolving film of Francois Odendaal's dream, came to me, crossed my path, inspired a reckless boldness, and one after another, introduced me to the nightmare I embraced. Loving the "river goddess" , I was affected differently by a system cracking at its seams, and would commit my life to a chilling passion. Without passion, my story would have ended with the credits rolling for Amazon.

If this were a story in the west, suffice to say, the inclusion of romance elicits spice, often encouraging skipping to the sections that steam off of the pages. It is not my intent to create such an event for page turning.

I hope through these pages the story will surprise the reader. To those who have experienced the fragile bearings of love, I offer a unique redemption. It has remained one for me.

CHAPTER 4
Teknikon

Later in the week after of our arrival, I walked from the hotel to Teknikon, my adjusted senses in the open, vibrating as if drawn with a bow over a violoncello's upper registers. The *con vivo* tempo marking suspended the Pretoria landscape above preconceptions of form and motif. I was happy to be a victim.

At Teknikon, college age students gathered in groups waiting for public transport. Their tempo marking was new, in contrast to my heightened intensity. Teknikon was to become the birthplace of all that governed my foray into madness, the source of what I would come to know as South Africa.

Teknikon was a technical occupational college offering training in auto mechanics, business, welding, music, art, drama, and film. I teach at the *Fame* school with a similar New York State teaching license, an occupational license in performing arts covering similar high school courses.

A special course, one offered only that month at Teknikon, would be taught to me by some students at the film school.

The architecture of Teknikon's one story building portrayed the role the English had during their colonial rule. The British Empire's inspired block shapes of brick, stone, and mortar left their history in South Africa in the name of the Queen. There was nothing new or remodeled, and if extended to imaginative reflection as one can do in a museum, stories of the various decades following the Boer Wars echoed in the hallways and classrooms.

Pretoria, 1986. The late 20th century disappeared. Time was more carefree, the uncomplicated life visible in the students. Boyish manhood mingled with shy, cautious girlhood. Idyllic climate, abundant food, and plenty of time to grow into adulthood yielded a healthy glow in the faces of the students I saw those first days in Pretoria. Womb-like, this alluring beauty created in me a wide eyed traveler bold to hunt for *Shangri-La,* a secret valley hidden from the world through imposed isolation and world condemnation.

Each day I passed the State Theater built by Afrikanerdom and the gold and diamonds. It felt unapproachable and had the same "off limits" that Lincoln Center warns to all unknown and aspiring artists. I passed by the State Theater on my way to Teknikon and then returned to the Burgerspark Hotel. I felt the thrill of being a nobody. Like Emily Dickinson's dying soldier hearing the trumpet of the enemy's victory, fame was my enemy, orchestral repertoire the poem's trumpet, and great performance halls and audiences my battlefield.

We are the world, we are the children..., a group of drama students at Teknikon sang, congregating near the film studio. I approached them.

"Excuse me. Why are you singing that song?" I asked.

In 1984, I had orchestrated an arrangement of *We are the World* for orchestra and chorus in order to raise money for the Ethiopian famine. A year prior to knowing I might travel to Africa, I composed Harvest Prelude for orchestra and boys choir set to a poem by Jamaican poet Sydney Hibbert who read for the premiere. The pop tune, *We are the World,* sung by South African students already had a history.

The students responded to me as wild deer often do in upstate New York, cautious as I held wild berries in my hand. A black student answered my question. There was a beautiful round mellifluousness in his accent.

"We are drama students," he responded. "We are going to tape this with the film students."

"May I observe?" I continued to boldly impose.

The instructor was cautious, but I volunteered my history working with students, and she granted my request.

Learning I was an American, the students wanted to know about our training, American feelings about boycott and sanctions, and careers in acting and film. It was odd being a spokesman for the entire American performing arts training and profession from the helm of a concert grand piano. The students listened politely. Their manner of speech, slower than mine with each variation of accent, charmed me. My star struck gaze must have been a curiosity to them. I felt like a gawking fool. This was their new image of the United States.

From these drama students, I heard the first strong statements condemning apartheid. They felt it was corrupt. The sooner apartheid ended, the better, even if this meant war and a bloodbath. Silence followed these words, offered by a white male drama student. Eyes went to the floor elsewhere, a far off look, a troubling quiet.

Due to sanctions, technology could not be upgraded for classroom instruction. Without appropriate training, these students would never be prepared to work in the capitals of the world. They learned as the blind learn, stumbling in the dark, feeling with their hands for the art their talents searched for. The truth was brutal. I was able to tell them only part of it. I thought about ways to get to them, particularly since they were at odds with the west through sanctions, and their society through opposing apartheid. It was a "no man's" land for these students.

This was OZ to me, however, and in that far off gaze in the eyes of these drama students judging apartheid, their exaggerated dreams were an Emerald City.

At the taping session I was placed in the sound booth. I sat next to a film student running the sound board. I had seen her earlier that morning tossing a frisbee to a classmate. Overthrowing it, landing near me, I picked it up tossing to her. Briefly, she studied me.

In the sound booth, she seemed to remember me. Where was I from? Why was I here? What was I looking for? Whatever it was, I would never find it among the Afrikaner men I worked with, she instructed. Had I been to Johannesburg? We were instructed to be quiet.

The resulting silence was potent. Something in her manner unbalanced me, timeless yet familiar. With each question from her the familiarity grew stronger. Like a mercurial winged messenger it evaded my grasp. Her words pierced the brick mortar of my history behind which lay childhood and carefree days. Her chatty, flute-like voice linked the spinning images of African bush to the images of boyhood that had made me a dreamer. Without thinking I spoke.

"Would you show me?"

"Maybe," she said with the same reserve she had had earlier accepting my return of the frisbee.

The session ended. I turned to leave the booth. Explosions crumbled the wall, and my childhood was overgrown with virgin forest.

"Could I have your phone number?"

After what seemed like a "no", she gave me a slip of paper.

Kathy Weir entered my days in South Africa carefully. She did so not as a lonely, unhappy female with hormonal imbalance charmed by a Casanova. I was a Martian, a visitor from another planet. I had an awkward manner of speech and walked too slowly. My thoughts to her seemed disconnected, but I listened well.

That evening at the Burgerspark Hotel I called her. When she walked into the lobby carrying her sandals in her hand, thus barefoot, the hotel personnel looked at her suspiciously. Her bare feet, a cotton summer dress, a colorful scarf pulling her hair back, her open ebullient face reminded me of a graceful Kudu ancestral spirit grazing in the Kalahari.

I instructed the staff to get me a cab. We took off for Jans Smuts International where I could rent a car in order to drive to Johannesburg. During the cab ride, my nerves created an aching body. This blurred my ability to make intelligent human conversation.

"Are you nervous?" she asked.

"Yes," I answered. It was the first coherent word from me. It wasn't the internal jail cell Philip Hattingh promised me, it was she. I resisted the impulse to jump out of the cab rolling into the safety of the high veld. The intensity was too much.

"You're schizophrenic," she remarked.

"No. I'm American," in response. My battered intelligence remained in the back seat of a Pretoria cab.

At the airport I struggled to get the cab fare from my pocket. My hands were shaking. Kathy Weir took the Rand and paid the fare certain I was impotent to do so.

Kathy Weir was in the company of a 35 year old emotional invalid.

"You could use a drink," she suggested.

At a bar in the terminal I ordered an Irish whiskey. Ah, mother's milk for any Irishman or Irish American! It turned my cauldron of disordered thoughts into clarity. A single question, very coherent came to me. It is the strong side of incoherent thought. Few could tolerate the rambling speech. In the United States, it was the age of first impressions and tight schedules.

In the rambling, an idea caught Kathy Weir's attention. The idea emerged out of a resurrection of ideas rushing into her world, a vast sea, an arc of the covenant carried by sails and wind of a divine spirit. Having to come though me, it squeaked into the late 20th Century into Kathy Weir's life.

She had been sharing with me her goal to become a filmmaker.

"There is an abundance of stories to be filmed in South Africa. I am concerned about what you are hearing in Pretoria. These men have macho attitudes. They live off of the backs of the black with maids and gardeners who for little pay provide them with comfortable lives."

"The black man must have their day. They must have their power, their country. You must be careful. Don't trust these men. They are very good at wining and dining foreigners. They will always paint their rosy picture of South Africa. I could tell when I first saw you that they had done so. You are very impressionable. Tonight, I will be your guide."

After a moment allowing me to take it in, she continued.

"I love South Africa, and will always love my country even if war comes, which at this point is likely."

Again there was the troubling quiet I experienced earlier from the drama students during the recording session. My hands shook again. I picked up my glass of whiskey. She stopped my arm waiting for my glance to meet hers.

"When you see the sun setting over Johannesburg, you will understand."

We were at the bar thirty minutes. Male war trophies faded. Kathy Weir, for her own reasons, loved me. Loving Kathy Weir, I loved her Africa.

My question emerged from this bond.

"If you could film a story here what would it be?"

Uncharacteristically, she became silent. She yielded to me. Her lovely eyes expressed a sudden exposed hunger. Not knowing she did so, she pulled me toward the dizzying images of African bush country. The seed planted by a bell hop's simple "thank you" my first moments at the Burgerspark Hotel, watered my question's soil, and I continued.

"Could this story alter suffering?"

She listened to her Africa far away from this airport bar. I continued.

"It must be a simple story. The greatest symphony, the most earth rattling novel, the record setting film sale, none will do. It must be a single idea. Honest, redemptive, radical, and, yes, inspiring. Unpretentious, innocent and naked."

She saw something. Whatever she saw, she kept it to herself.

In the days that followed, Kathy Weir eventually found the courage or recklessness to sleep with me one evening. We were like children at a sleep over. We lay side by side talking about an art that could change everything. When we finally went to sleep, she was holding me.

She never revealed what she had seen the evening at the airport bar.

That evening in Johannesburg, we walked emptied streets. I took her hand, breathing the late African summer air, mindlessly looking at store windows. I felt a boyhood peace.

A bomb went off in a government building, the first of many that would result in the government declaring a national state of emergency. Thousands would be jailed or worse, secretly executed. Harsh reality spit on my redemptive story.

The delicate breezes that evening quieted my spinning images of Africa into a softer blur, in which voices sang a music interwoven with the violence crying for redemption. In the midst was the South African nightmare.

Kathy Weir filled me with a passion for South Africa. The evening she did so, she also began to fade from my grasp or any potential intimacy. I was being pulled back. Our lives were not star crossed, but were instead a beautiful accident, one the result of Americans who were uninvited bullying our way into these lives. Through this accident I was with one of Africa's true daughters. For a time my life belonged to Kathy Weir.

Later that evening in Johannesburg at 2 am, we went into a bar on Rocky Street. Huddled in a corner surrounded by attentive friends, I met Kathy Weir's future lover, Paul Myburgh.

Together we would one day film a simple story in Soweto. In Soweto I would hear the music. I walked with Kathy Weir, blurred by magic that was Kathy Weir's Africa, my state of bliss that evening . Only in Soweto would I understand.

CHAPTER 5
Die Bruderbond

Carl Theunissen told me that he needed an entire day in order to explain South African history. Otherwise, he did not want to discuss it. He was brash and used to it. He was the bush-wise, high veld Afrikaner the western capitals despised. Defeated by the British during the Boer Wars, the Afrikaner had been dealt cruel blows from the British Empire, their farms burned to the ground, their wives and children imprisoned in camps dying by the thousands. The brilliant horse back riding Afrikaner, the first to refine guerilla warfare strategies, formed a "brotherhood" or Bruderbond that in time rose in power, voted into government control, and established apartheid, the word for "separation" in Afrikanse.

Many Afrikaner children grew up on farms side by side with black children as playmates, thus speaking Afrikanse as well as Zulu, Xhosa, or other Bantu tongues. In adulthood the laws of separation enforced a division, thus friend to friend became "baas".

I learned none of this from Carl Theunissen. I have my own theory why; language. Carl and other Afrikaners I met hated to speak English. They had been forced to learn it under British rule.

Afrikaners often remarked that Afrikanse had a poetry and syntax English lacked. The Afrikaner poets were held in high esteem, similar to the honored place Russians gave their poets. Their history in Afrikanse was told within poetic rhythms and moods. English was too flat, too unmusical, too limited.

Carl Theunissen had heard about Jack's arrival in South Africa, and had asked Philip Hattingh to arrange a meeting. The Afrikaner braaivleis traditionally set the atmosphere for business meetings. The barbecue was somewhat like a braaivleis. African game was cooked in the open with other meats, washed down with beer, all in substantial amounts. The open air in Africa welcomed a large appetite. The girth and height of Afrikaner men justified their appetite. Black's also favored the braaivleis, and beef jerky was the recreational choice snack food of all races.

Carl's film studio was located halfway between Johannesburg and Pretoria, a single storied complex standing alone among windmills, open spaced farmland, slightly hilly, watched over silently, yet unpredictably by African weather patterns ranging from ten year droughts to earth rattling thunderstorms.

Jack and Carl were discussing film. I looked across the open field and watched black laborers walking down an unpaved road. Carl saw me watching them. Spilling a portion of his beer, he stormed over to the fence yelling at them in Afrikanse.

What the hell had they done? The sound of his voice was fierce and full of hostility. I felt disgusted, and turned towards Jack to suggest we leave.

Suddenly, the laborers were laughing, pointing their fingers at Carl Theunissen, and bending to the waist slapping their thighs.

He walked back to us glaring at me with a sly smile on his face. He sat down, picked up his beer, downed it, opened another, and looked at me.

"I can see it will take TWO days in order to explain South African history to you!" This laugh included Jack Jourgensen's.

After my initiation into Afrikaner history I was excused. Carl and Jack argued about film making the rest of the afternoon. Their attempts to dominate each other were loud enough to be heard everywhere.

Alone and humiliated I walked away to find a quiet place in Afrikanerdom. I opened a screened door and entered a room. Theunissen's secretary was there. Petra smiled and invited me to sit with her. She had witnessed my history lesson. Plump, very pretty as well as very voluptuous, she was also a very young 19.

She rose from her chair coming to stand near me. I shook her hand. It was clammy. She spoke with shy glances darting but bright with infatuation. I could hear Jack and Carl's voices dominating the countryside. I looked out the window towards the sound of the voices.

"Carl likes you a great deal. He would not have done what he did otherwise, Patrick. You must try and not be hurt."

She moved closer to me. She positioned herself allowing me to come closer. I felt free to look at her without speaking, feeling comfortable while she smiled warmly. Permission was granted, but I remained seated with my cupped hands holding my knee. She accepted my civil caution.

Towards evening Jack and I prepared to leave. I shook Petra's hand. She held my hand for a long time, until I ended the handshake. She looked at me with sadness. Jack and I drove to the unpaved road turning right onto the road. I looked back. Against the backdrop of an approaching thunderstorm the silhouetted figure of Petra stood silently watching us.

In the distance, Carl Theunissen's studio looked like a farmhouse. The winds of an imminent storm blew the windmill. Die Bruderbond wined and dined Jack and me. Kathy Weir was right. Carl was very good at it. He was too busy with Jack to notice what really happened.

I looked back once more. Petra walked away into the darkness of the African dusk.

CHAPTER 6
A Lecture

"Choose carefully a subject. Then embrace the tedium required to bring it to life. Avoid being cheap, for instance, by imitation. At this time here in South Africa each of you have a unique opportunity not afforded my students. You cannot afford to waste creativity."

Fanie Van der Merve had asked me to lecture on the subject of film music. Fanie was the head of the film school at Teknikon. Accompanying Francois Odendaal on the river expeditions, he had filmed the dreams of his countryman. From the top of Mt. Everest to canoeing the arctic Alaskan waters, through both Amazon journeys and Patagonia he was a legend among his aspiring film students.

My first day at Teknikon I looked him up. At first cautious, he warmed when I introduced myself. Francois had sent a special request to Fanie that he make a special effort to welcome me. Smiling, he told me he had heard good things about me.

He had a rugged handsomeness, twinkling eyes set in a sun baked face, speaking with a measured rhythm, probably the result of a love for Afrikanse. His girl students had already asked him about me. To this he warmly approved, and insisted I must enjoy the attention. In fact, he had already arranged an evening hosted by him that would give these girls a chance to meet me. If I was available that evening, he would pick me up at the hotel.

27

That evening, expecting only Fanie, in his small Italian sports car were the collection of film students wishing to meet me. I climbed in the front seat next to Fanie. The back seat was filled with smiling faces stacked on laps. We arrived at a restaurant sports bar. Since South Africa still had the British Empire's habit of keeping to the left side, the stairwell to the restaurant filled with people exiting thus. My western habit keeping to the right received some angry impatient glances. One of Fanie's students pulled me into the left lane of traffic.

As the honored guest, I was asked many questions about American life style, dating, and being famous. From these I learned how influential the American culture was, and I felt a need to impress upon them the unique role they had in South Africa. Fanie, who had lived for a time in Los Angeles, understood and approved. He clearly respected me for not using male bravado, American career style in order to win these lovely girls.

Since the evening was too short and casual for in-depth discussion, Fanie the next day at Teknikon, asked me to give a lecture for the film school.

I was nervous at the lecture, smoking my pipe (when I could successfully light it with shaking hands), and covering a wide spectrum of music in film.

Sir Leo Arnaud was my major source for film music. Born in Lyon, France, he had as a 21 year old, instructed Maurice Ravel, at Ravel's invitation, on the form and style of American jazz. Leo became Maurice Chevalier's music director, convincing Chevalier to sing in English, the turning point for Chevalier's career. Coming on boat to the United States he played with and arranged for American jazz greats before going to Hollywood where he joined the staff of MGM as composer, orchestrator, and arranger for over 300 motion pictures scoring for Fred Astaire, Judy Garland, and for one of the Marx Brother's films, among many others. From a collection of fanfares he did for Capitol Records, ABC picked up a section that became the famous Olympic Fanfare. Everyone learned from Leo in Hollywood including André Previn and John Williams. I was his last pupil, he my mentor and musical father. He died with me and his wife, Faye, next to him.

With our pipes lit, and a glass of red wine, we studied music. I absorbed "tricks", as he called them, and stories of his long life mixed with the treasure he owned from years of mastery. This is worth its own book, since there are stories that will die with me otherwise.

The lecture went past the time Fanie gave me. The classroom was filled with alert minds, hungry for my real stories. Questions followed. They were challenging. American superficiality packaged in technology making our market rule the world seemed to them both a point of admiration and a potential downfall. The American culture bullied the world with its films.

Their hunger forced me to reflect on my own goals. In South Africa, where I was lecturing on American film, there was a war that was both civil as well as foreign. Conflicts raged on the borders of Namibia with Angola. Aware of this, I listened to their criticism of the vast amounts of American dollars spent weekly on a tv show at the time, Miami Vice.

The combination took me back to the "60's", when art was created for social causes. My own days in South Africa had taken on a timelessness. Their dreams ascended into a blinding harsh light, a reality bending into a prism made all the more potent by these students' fertile minds. I felt inept. I had no answers. Along with their isolation from sanctions my silence remained hovered above the heads of the students. It was an awkward moment.

I stepped outside to light my pipe. I heard a din of conversation back in the classroom. When I returned, they listened for my answer.

" You talented young people are losing something. What you could be profoundly expressing is being drained by this South African 'good life'. Please accept this as only an opinion. It is an opinion from one who is at the present very confused."

29

I looked across the room at the faces of these students. A girl sat quietly off to one side. She looked at me. I had never seen a face whose eyes reflected some other world's torment as transparent as hers. She was also a face, one of the most beautiful I had ever seen looking back at me with an S.O.S.

Soon, through her life, I would be introduced to the nightmare of South Africa. Through her I would come to know the one in my own soul.

CHAPTER 7
Veronique

She was from Cape Town. The tip of the African continent, a city surrounded by nature's table, a mountain covered often with a fog that draped the rock as a table cloth drapes a table. Table Mountain, Cape Town, and 500 miles away Antarctica. The Indian ocean's warm water meets head on the cold waters of the Atlantic. Storms unlike any other in world waters chased sailors into oblivion over the centuries.

Here in this part of the world nature graced Veronique with both its beauty and its nature. As rare as its beauty and its intensity, a natural world created a girl whose facial features in years to come would grow into the handsome features worn well from courageous living. She was as much a goddess as the African winds create when life begins at first daylight, hunts, feeds, procreates, and at dusk fades without judgment day, passing to a new generation of African life, owned by none.

In contrast, I came from a society where ownership began and ended each day with the first light. Days passed without regard to that fresh beginning. My life shared the same rhythm, and for that I loved constrained by limits. I carried these with me to Africa, careful to not leave hurt and pain behind. My cupped hands listening to Petra, the contentment to hold Kathy Weir's heart, and the choice to keep in tow my feelings for others who loved my adventure, I would partake up to the limits mandated by ownership.

Only once, and the consequences paid the price, did I become what I came into this war torn society to avoid, namely the nature that composing music kept in check.

After my lecture at the film school, Fanie Van der Merwe offered a dinner at a French restaurant outside Pretoria. Originally, Jack Jourgensen was to join us. He had asked Veronique to accompany him, changing his mind at the last minute. He had a meeting in Johannesburg.

Fanie was annoyed. He asked me whether I minded if Veronique joined us. I told him I would personally ask her if she would join me when I saw her.

Later that day while sitting outside the editing room in the quad, I saw Veronique near the public pay phone. She looked my way. Sunlight lit her strong countenance framed by South Africa's tenacious summer heat. I informed her there had been a change of plans, and I asked whether she would join me instead. She listened unhurriedly. I felt awkward. She smiled.

"Lovely," she responded.

She turned to complete her phone call.

I was 35. With one word, "lovely", I left behind ownership. I became aware of a different maturity out of bounds of discipline, a maturity flowering in nightmares, a madness infecting me with realities found in war. With Veronique and through her, my embryonic faith in the African dawn would come into the world an infant.

When the evening approached, Fanie came by the Burgerspark hotel leaving Veronique with me while he drove to pick up his girlfriend. Alone with me she was comfortable. It was as though we had met before and could dispense with obligatory conversations. When Fanie returned, Veronique sat with me in the back seat. She was unguarded, open, and unafraid of close physical contact.

At the restaurant the topic of conversation centered around failed dreams. Fanie lived for a time in Los Angeles and knew the American tendency to inflate stories in order to make a good impression. Again, he appreciated the fact that I did not.

Veronique remained quiet. Occasionally she would take my cigarette from the ash tray and take a drag. Then she returned it to my hand.

A pianist played near us. I in courtesy to him waived playing when asked. When he left, the request renewed. I played. Already some new music came from the piano extemporaneous to the presets of my repertoire. I was surprised watching my hands find notes. When asked what the music was, I could only falter with an "I'm not sure?" I made it up? Something else played me. Had it happened before? No, it had not. "You Americans are the best technically." But this had nothing to do with technique!

Leaving the restaurant walking in the gardens towards the car, Veronique put her arm through mine.

"You play beautifully. You won me."

I tried to explain. She pulled my arm closer to her.

"I assure you, I understand," she said.

There was singing near Fanie's car. A group of young men were out and about celebrating the marriage the following day of their friend. They came up to us in high spirits offering a swig of wine from a shared bottle. Fanie responded in Afrikanse. What he said increased their spirit of revelry. They shook his hand and ran off into the garden.

Driving to Fanie's apartment, he returned to the car with a bottle of champagne. He gunned his sports car and drove to the gardens near the government buildings of Pretoria. It was illegal to be there at that hour. We ran into the garden filled with indigenous flowers of southern Africa.

Opening the champagne we drank while Fanie pointed out the Southern Cross in the cloudless night sky. This constellation had been a guide for sailors over the centuries. In that late hour, the scents from the garden's flowers in bloom mingled with the view of this hemisphere's stars. Veronique quietly sat, her legs folded under her, leaning on her arm. Unless spoken to, she looked at the ground, her beauty silhouetted against the bluish night. Beneath the four of us was the African soil, a soil that could be a tyrant. That evening she was at rest. We sat on this great

33

whale's back, a giant who could and had erupted violently, mercilessly erasing lives of men from the most important to the humblest. Even in the lateness of the hour I was wide awake.

We left for the drive to take Veronique home. When we pulled up in front of her house, Fanie pulled me aside.

"Wave me off if you decide to stay," he confided.

Once in her house, I decided to go with the music that had played me. I waved him off. Fanie's tires burned rubber in the dead quiet of the night.

Veronique frantically tried to stop him.

Once Fanie was gone, she resigned to my aggressive act. She offered me some tea. I watched her in her kitchen, essence of a dancer's grace preparing the tea pot with the cups on a tray. Returning, she knelt at my feet and poured my tea. She leaned against my leg sipping hers. Her beautiful, dark, sad eyes betrayed her pain. Even so her countenance gleamed. I wondered what the source of her tragedy was. She trembled. Her glances often would erupt with unsteady lightening. Her laughter had a sorrow in its timbre.

Once we finished drinking the tea, she suggested I sleep on the couch. I could in no way accept the offer.

"I don't think so," I responded gently.

She took my hand and led me to her room. She left to prepare for bed. There was a simple mattress on the floor in her room. On her walls were photographs of apartheid victims. Who took the pictures, I wondered? Who did she know, and where had she been? The window in the bedroom was open, late hour breezes came into the room from a dead quiet outside.

The music from the piano returned in my memory. Everything was playing me. I was in a new world away from all I depended on for a compass. I looked out the window and found the Southern Cross again. Where was I?

Veronique came into the room quietly. She was dressed in a simple cloth gown. She lay in her bed, and looked at me. There was no resistance in her gaze. It was for me to walk towards her without a compass.

34

I stood over her near the mattress on the floor. As she sat up, I undraped her simple cotton gown. She looked at me comfortable in her nakedness. There was no more sorrow in her countenance only a warm directed strength, a deep passionate caring reflecting her confidence in what she needed and what she would take to calm the heat from living in a society that was her enemy.

The bluish African night filled the room through the open window as I descended into its shadows. Within that fluid hour consciousness disappeared.

It was forbidden fruit. Sweet to the taste, bitter to the soul. Her loneliness became mine. I walked out of the garden of Eden and the safety of Pretoria, losing the rhythms of love in the wilderness' primal darkness; oppression. I heard the redemptive sounds again of Africa's music, a celestial music similar to what I imagine frightened shepherds heard when the infant Jesus lay in an innocent girl's arms. Joys and agonies bounced off a river canyon's wall, and I heard faintly the busy everyday bustle of children's voices back in the real world. If you understand, come...

Into my flesh, passed from Veronique's, was the anger for a society that created apartheid. The hatred flew into the Southern Cross, thrust after thrust of her body pounding the earth beneath us, joined man to woman, a daughter of Africa who had paid the price of sanity in order to deny the savage oppression of a majority.

Only a few hours before morning I slept. I drifted into a sleep that was Africa's.

I awoke to someone knocking at her door. Startled, she told me to quickly dress and climb out the window. It was at that point she told me she had a boyfriend. He was at her door.

I dressed. I climbed out the window and met her at the back door.

"In a few days, I will come to you again," she said.

There was a street. I had no clue where to go. Walking towards any bus stop, two Africans sat on the grass as I passed.

"Hey! Man! You're a musician," they yelled at me.

I walked to them asking how they knew.

"Because, brother, we are musicians! A musician knows a musician," they answered.

"Do you know our music? You must learn our music. During the day we work for very few Rands, but at night! At night we go out and make music. To know South Africa you must learn our music, my brother."

I promised them I would do so. Whatever played me the night before at the restaurant, and stayed with me through the night buried with Veronique, now appeared at first light in the form of two African musicians. In this morning light, accompanied by the Transvaal's aviary, Veronique's madness became mine. These musicians played their music at night, and I assumed once I discovered their music, sanity would return.

Meanwhile, my breathing was in short gasps, I perspired heavily, and struggled to find bearings to the Burgerspark Hotel. I had tasted violence and yearned for righteousness.

Veronique. South African musicians. My first introduction to the true nightmare in South Africa. A young woman resisting apartheid, tortured inside with pain and isolation. Black musicians living beyond pain, enduring the day until at night they lived in their music.

Veronique kept her promise. For two days I paced in my hotel room shaken and disheveled. I avoided the Amazon team. I was not enduring well what I was having to face in myself, nor what I now saw in South Africa.

We ate dinner at the hotel. She sat near me, her legs wrapped in mine under the table. She was curious about my life. She said she did not believe such a life was possible for her in South Africa.

She shared her feelings about her country, her friends in the midst of opposing apartheid. She especially loved Cape Town.

"Apartheid must end. The blacks must have their country. Your lecture at the film school was inspiring but I feel wasted on those students. It is too easy being white. I was asked to run for Miss South Africa. I turned it down so that my family would not be attacked if I expressed my views. When I take the train from Cape Town to school, I often ride in the black section. It can be quite dangerous. These people only see a white girl, not one who is for their rights to govern."

I asked her why she opened to me.

"You are unpredictable and dangerous, my dear. I get too easily bored."

Was I a distraction?

"No. You are a life."

Later we went to my room. Alone, she wanted to again forget and "live". For two days a storm had been threatening in me. In her love making the storm erupted and the violent soil of the great whale shattered the last vestiges of reason. It was the beginning of the many days that have followed in my life that have measured me unstable or mad among those to which I have returned. Thus I burned the western-destiny bridge, never able to look back.

Veronique disappeared from pain, politics, commitment. No rules. No apartheid. In her cry was the freedom of pleasure. She threw herself off the cliff of this gulag Afrikanerdom that had plowed from her own soil, ripping the ripe crops of apartheid from the ground before they had time to root in her. Apartheid turned her emotional fires into vast fields of mud, and she required her lovers to roll in it with her.

In time there was a quiet in the room. She was sleeping peacefully. I sat at the end of the bed watching her. She opened her eyes and smiled. Coming towards me, we sat at the foot of the bed.

A terror suddenly gripped her. I saw the nightmare return. Like Orpheus I had looked back and lost her to Hades. My instinct was to run. I had already endured two days of a threatening storm, another one I had no endurance for, particularly one I did not understand. My faculties for reason had left me the first night with her.

Instead of running, I held her. Across continents, languages, democracies, dictatorships, taxes, schools, Vietnam's, Ethiopian famines, property ownership, I begged her to look at me .

I waited. She became calmer. "I love you, Veronique."

Old warm and fuzzy meanings were replaced with anger at injustice, a fire demanding righteousness. I would love South Africa radically altered.

I drifted into sleep. Veronique's image was the last before I fell asleep. She stood unclothed in front of the mirror lit with the mirror's light in an otherwise dark room. She was combing her long black hair. She was silhouetted in the darkness as she had been the night in the gardens.

Early morning I quietly left to go with Fanie to a game farm. She was still asleep. When I returned later in the day there was a note from Veronique.

"We exhaust each other, my dear."

Jack Jourgensen asked Veronique to be the river goddess in Amazon. I was in Johannesburg when they shot her for the film. Kathy Weir and I were recording voice over for the film. I don't think the Amazon crew wanted me there. School was out. Veronique needed the money from the shoot in order to get home to Cape Town.

She had asked where I was. They told her.

Amazon would air in the United States on the Discovery Channel. The first image seen in the documentary was Veronique, the river goddess... I am the river, I will always be the river, if you understand...come.

CHAPTER 8
Learn our music!

I joined Kathy Weir one evening at the Market Theater in Johannesburg. The first all black-acted and black-produced play in South Africa, Bopha, was having its first run. This theater was founded by Athol Fugard, the playwright whose play, Master Harold and the Boys, I had been introduced to at the Missouri Repertory Theater in Kansas City. There was a vitality in the market life. An East Village sister except that under the apartheid system, government censorship was only blocks away in central Jo'burg.

Cultures mixed, particularly among the young. Art and music flourished both in the stalls on market day as well as inside the theater complex, buildings more like warehouses than any upscale theater space. Kathy loved the Market.

Kathy Weir had taken my 35 mm camera one day, and with Paul Myburgh, taken pictures that would allow me to see the Market through their perspective. Paul was enchanted with Kathy Weir. There was an immediacy in their lives, while at the same time there was inconsistency in mine. Kathy loved me. I knew that this would remain a constant throughout her life. Those days in South Africa I could promise no more than a memory, albeit an enchanted one. Paul could do otherwise for her.

Bopha had a cast of four actors. The plot centered around blacks employed as policemen. The pay and security dwarfed all other employment opportunities for blacks. The exchange for this security was doing surreptitious police work, on behalf of maintaining apartheid, which compromised family and friend.

The theater space was the size of an off off Broadway house. A mixed audience filled the 90 or more seats. Some of the dialogue was in Afrikanse, the language blacks were mandated to learn in school. To my surprise, humor drove the plot forward in those sections of the play in Afrikanse. I had no clue as to the meaning of the words that created the responsive laughter.

It was clear that there would be no censorship of a play that brought laughter from an audience. Moved to tears at the play's end, and the only one moved so, the play revealed the issues of the human heart chained to a brutal separation of a people from the same community, black against black.

It was the first time that I heard South African acapella song, another device that moved the plot forward.

The songs resisted strong downbeats, staying on the other side of the first beat of the bar. The shapes of phrases bounced in between common time's square meter. The music laughed. When it was militant, it had joy. There was no sorrow. No blues. Actors danced in song, the body swayed in one direction as the phrase of music went another. I wanted to dance with them.

Kathy Weir bounced in her seat. She nudged me.

"I must teach you to dance, Paddy!"

Our first night together, returning to Pretoria from Hillbrow, I asked her to stay a while. I took her to the dining area where a piano sat in the corner. Moving it out to the patio, I sat her next to me. I played. The mysterious new music was there in its infancy. Added to the fragile melodic textures was the effect Africa had made on my music. I watched my hands go to places shaped now by rhythmic joy. Kathy softened. I didn't want to stop. Western music requires a coda and a double bar, so it spattered to an end.

"What was that?" she asked.

Again I did not know.

Something else played the music. She stood up and took my hand. She led me to the grassy garden area near the patio. Placing my hand on her back, her hand on my shoulder, she moved towards me in a quick sharp step.

"This is the tango. Relax."

I faltered the tango with Kathy Weir in the early morning hours in Pretoria, South Africa. It is the dance of conquest, resisted by the female, until she yields to the male in total submission. Following a brief moment when Kathy Weir had given me a tango's permission, I walked her to the lobby and ordered a cab.

The next day we went to a record store in order to find music I knew. A closed room, some broken ear phones that had to be held to the ears, and a recording of Chopin's piano works introduced Kathy to my life.

"Do you hear how Chopin plays with music? I hear this same quality in African song. He drew from the folk music of Poland. He left his country and sadly missed it his entire life. I have been thinking about this a great deal. I'm wondering whether African musicians would like to create a classical music from their music. I, for one, would be inspired and altered by such a music."

This idea did not make sense to her. She felt African music was complete. Why westernize it?

"I'm hoping the west would be "Africanized" by this music."

This was an inspiring idea to her, but she felt that without Africans who knew what I knew, it was unlikely.

"What if I introduced a work I've composed about Africa here in concert? I have a work for orchestra and boys choir called Harvest Prelude. It has a poem by a Jamaican poet. The idea could be introduced this way. I would be honest. It is not African."

She embraced the idea that I would share my art with her country. African or not.

The South African Symphony lived at the State Theater. That imposing complex would have to be my way in which to enter and gain access to musicians and a conductor. How would I begin?

Amazon was finished. Jack Jourgensen was preparing to return to the US. I shared with him my idea for a performance of Harvest Prelude. Jack had recorded the performance back in the US. He believed I had a worthy mission and suggested I remain for a few more weeks in order to visit the State Theater. When Jack left he left me a note wishing me well.

My first attempts were thwarted by the usual resistance symphonies have for drop ins. I was politely told that their seasons were billed far in advance. My detailed description of the music and the role it could play in South Africa fell on deaf ears. To be fair, a classical orchestra resists any new music, particularly music with a mission.

I spent some time with Philip Hattingh. I filled him in on my quest and the failure thus far.

"You were with the SABC crowd. They never get anything right. Look, let me go through my office at tourism. We are a lot brighter, and can see a bigger picture. I think your boys choir should be a children's choir with candles lit for the performance. We can make it happen."

Philip worked as an editor for South African Tourism, which in 1986 was having a slump due to sanctions and boycotts. Certainly an orchestra piece by an American composer that gave a different view of South Africa would be something tourism would bend an ear to.

Thus this story truly begins. Veronique's dark passion , Kathy Weir's beautiful innocent love of her country and me, and Philip Hattingh's tempting door for me to find a way Harvest Prelude could be performed; this scenario established the story board for what was to come.

It seems obvious perhaps that I should have called it a day. What business did an American have doing business in South Africa under international boycotts? These exact words were written to me in a letter from Senator Ted Kennedy following my first visit while looking for support for my idea. Only a madman would play on both sides of a dangerous political conflict and risk his life for an idea no one understood.

Yet, the story continued. Africa could only be experienced in Africa. I have seen it in the eyes of anyone who has been there. I have also seen the vacant looks from those who have not been to Africa when I describe the sun, the air, and the night sky.

My thoughts blurred into this euphoria when the South African 747 left for New York City. It was a crowded plane. I looked out of the window as we ascended. The sun was setting.

"When you see the sun setting over Johannesburg, then you will understand," Kathy Weir had said to me our first night together, the evening she and her sun had become a part of me.

I left a note on the bulletin board at the film school; "I will return."

I was returning home. My studio, pencils, manuscripts, operas, symphonies.

Nothing would be the same again.

EPILOGUE TO PART I

And the composer and the country in conflict lived happily ever after. The reader. Who is this? Someone with a critical eye finding gaping holes in a dime store fantasy. Someone hungry for escape willing to buy into the journey through a war in Oz.

Years have passed. My romanticism in those days has settled into Jack Jourgensen's reality. A fifty year old man often views the world through less adventure. Reading the journal from a thirty year old man, I tug at the bit, knowing that I was lost then, the proverbial ship without a rudder, ignoring the suffering, caught up in a seed of an idea created solely from the spinning universe, not the practical earth where the rich get richer, etc., etc.

Had I been a black American composer, or any other race than white, this would be a far more compelling tale. I would have been received far differently, and seen the side nearer the truth. Instead, I have in this book a young man's adventure that is flawed because it is written by a middle aged witness. There was abundant evidence of flaws throughout my journey. I chose to ignore them. I am not able to do so now. The reader I keep addressing, in fact, is mostly myself.

I would like to end this book with Part One. Doing so leaves memory in gentler climes. Once the machinery of the powerful Afrikaner infrastructure befriended me, my journey to Oz darkened. The large self-created set design, piece by piece, dismantled. No one was interested in the play I wrote. With few exceptions, the African Mozart lived in my head alone. I am sure that for many of the people reading this who are in the story, the The African Mozart as the theme would surprise them. Each of them had their own reason for involving hours of their lives in mine.

To apologize for writing is self defeating. In a book on South Africa during the apartheid years, not to do so, is unjust and opportunistic. This dilemma drains life from my story, and draining the life, the reader closes the book.

What does invigorate the reader is passion kept alive from stories remembered in the course of friendships and love. Behind the poetic phrases liberally and literally drawn from the original journal lies heartache. The shape relies on symphonic form rather than book form. This journey through Africa, the symphony, I listen to as though it was yesterday.

What follows has no requirement for a book critic. The fears, defeat, and remarkable beauty need only symphonic development, recapitulation and the coda. This criticism belongs in the domain of the musician. In my approaching autumn years this music's story remains joyful.

Mahler's Resurrection symphony, Mendelssohn's Trio in D minor, the recordings of the Soweto String Quartet, and my song cycle, Music for Friends based on my years in South Africa live in these pages. In that context it is a 20th century counterpoint, dissonant, struggling for African form in the shadow of the giants of 19th century romanticism.

CHAPTER 9
Back Home and Changed

The western press reported escalated violence between the South African government and the ANC resistance. Images of the conflict moved South African censorship forward, and the western press complained. Sanctions moved forward at the same time. Any friendly eye towards South Africa labeled an individual or American corporation supporters of apartheid, subject to potential prosecution. A composer with a vision to find a classical African music was not exempt. My appeal to Senator Edward Kennedy on behalf of a cultural peace making venture was dismissed as detrimental to sanctions. The letter was signed by him.

I was not to be deterred.

I made a phone call to Graham Martin within a month of my return. He supported enthusiastically my works as a composer. I often played my music in private soirees where a distinguished audience listened attentively. Among them were business leaders, writers, performers, choreographers, actors, and pseudo-aristocrats.

I knew who Graham was, but never knew his past or views based on his life as an American ambassador. The first person to offer any light on his place in American diplomatic service was a writer at one of the soirees. His name I have, unfortunately, forgotten. The evening I spoke with him, I had finished playing the piano and gone to the bar for a drink. He stood apart from the crowd observing rather than participating in chitchat. I introduced myself.

He was in town in order to interview Graham Martin. The Vietnam war was Graham's debacle. He had taken the assignment, Richard Nixon pleading with him against Graham's better judgment. Until Vietnam, Graham had served as ambassador to Thailand where because of his policies with Thailand's king, Thailand remained the gateway to the free world in Asia.

Graham related to me a story. He had insisted the US military build roads reaching the northern boundaries of Thailand where communists from neighboring countries had access. With good roads, food could easily get to the poor. Without hunger, the communists could not get a foothold. The US military balked at the assignment to build roads. Graham ordered them as the arm of the presidency to do so. If he was not obeyed, the military would be thrown out of Thailand. The roads were built.

Vietnam was not so easy. When Graham arrived, the US escalated the bombing with the north, erasing jungle foliage with agent orange. It was the height of carnage, the press images as troubling as the images in the future coming from South Africa.

The evening of the soiree the writer expressed his opinion that Graham Martin was one of the last truly great American heroes. He commented looking around the room that he doubted anyone present at that gathering knew. He was writing a comprehensive book on the Vietnam conflict. He felt that Graham had taken the weight of the fall, and that it was unmerited. Henry Kissinger's Paris negotiations stalled the eventual downfall of the South Vietnamese US backed and subsequent US deserted government. The eventual murder of thousands of Vietnamese who had trusted America grieved Graham Martin. Once the fraudulent peace failed, Graham returned to the US and faced Congress as the target of antiwar wrath.

I eventually called Graham. Intimidated, I had stared at his phone number a good while before dialing. His wife, Dorothy, answered. Soon I heard his voice. Would he see me? " Of course," he replied.

At his home he invited me in. We met in his study. On the coffee table were scattered periodicals, newspapers, and a tape recorder. He kept the tape recorder whenever there were interviews. Misquoting him was a major concern.

I went into detail relating my journey to South Africa. He listened. Suffering from imphezema, a tube led from his nose to the oxygen tank. Graham was tall, over six feet, and handsome with the carriage of a leader. He allowed me to talk without interruption. I was nervous.

When I finished, he was silent for a time before responding.

"You have a worthy mission," he finally said.

I informed him that seeking exemption from sanctions I had written Senator Ted Kennedy hoping he would share my vision of peace.

Laughing at my quandary he shared a story.

"When I was serving in the administration of President John F. Kennedy, I was often in the oval office with the President. During one of these meetings, an assistant interrupted to report a sticky situation in Mexico involving the President's brother, Ted. He had been arrested found naked in a fountain. President Kennedy looked over his reading glasses towards me and remarked, 'There is a bad apple in every family'."

Clearly Graham felt Ted Kennedy was not someone to be taken seriously. I was not in the position to be as bold and certainly did not want to break a law. Graham pointed out to me that I was not exchanging dollars. I had a project mutually beneficial to both parties in conflict. It was a project he humorously suggested that both the US and South African governments would "wonder what rock this guy crawled out from under".

Graham insisted care must be taken when dealing with South Africa. He compared it to riding on the back of a tiger. A worthy mission such as mine could polarize the best intentions and be misused for political gain. Either side could, in fact, make such a mission dangerous to me, and more likely, dangerous to my family. While music remained the universal language, by principle, a language of peace, hymns raised temperatures. Many a nation had gone to war with the stanza of national pride.

If I found the African Mozart, who would claim the genius, and for what purpose? The National Party could be supportive of the discovery in order to soften their image to the world. The ANC could embrace the young genius as long as this young lion acknowledged the chains from which the art must free others. An American insisting such a talent belonged to neither, but carried the bridges of reconciliation for all could prove idealistic and problematic.

It was clear to Graham that I wanted to ride the tiger's back.

He expressed the opinion that since I had achieved interest to date from so many people it meant success I should not underrate. Many would come and go from fear. Success would guarantee more to come on board. Failure meant equally many might jump ship. I must not carry personal grudges against those who jumped ship, and in fact, include them once again if their courage returned. "Maintain a healthy cynicism. The success of your mission outweighs personal feelings."

He shared with me an old adage. Success has many fathers. Failure is an orphan.

"Many want credit for a success. Allow it. Giving away credit will guarantee others joining. Keep a slow pace. Don't be too eager to get results. Polarization will be limited by taking a cautious route. Without careful assessment, each day's critical situation could escalate into a misunderstanding resulting in a serious miscalculation. There are many dead men from a government's miscalculated assessment of one man's threat."

"You will probably not in your lifetime see a fruitful outcome," he continued. "Many years might pass before an African Mozart fulfills the destiny you envision. Be satisfied with the many who might embrace the vision. It is its own success."

He admitted that he had given up receiving credit or acknowledgment for his work. He had been surprised in recent years from the accolades he was receiving for his life's work.

He illustrated his point that one must remain cynical with a rare discussion of his last days in Saigon. The evacuation of American troops and personnel proved grave personal danger for Graham and his staff.

Last to leave the embassy, he loaded one by one people onto a Marine helicopter on the roof of the embassy. The North Vietnamese Army converged on Saigon preparing to enter the city. Graham referred to 'playing a poker hand' dealing with the crisis. He asked his assistant to get the general of the Vietcong forces on the phone. Speaking to the general, Graham warned him that if they entered Saigon before every American was evacuated, the US Naval fleet in the harbor would blow them into eternity. In truth, there was no such fleet. Americans were successfully evacuated. He won his hand on the bluff.

He was the last to leave the embassy. Of great personal sadness to him was the large numbers of Vietnamese personnel working for the Americans left behind at the end of the war.

Graham felt that it was very important to document my mission in a film. Here he warned me of even greater dangers. "Get the film in the can without press interviews. Otherwise, others to their advantage could edit to their own specified political agendas," he warned.

What about censoring what I filmed?

"Film whatever they want," he replied. "Film what you want, too."

He related another story to make his point.

During World War II, Graham worked in Washington for the consulate services. He was assigned to accompany filmmaker, Frank Capra, who was shooting a propaganda film for the army. He had an appointment to film General George Patton in the general's office. Mr. Capra was directed by the general what to shoot and at what angles. Graham watched, surprised by Frank Capra's yielding to the general's artistic tyranny.

Once the filming was over, outside the general's office, Graham asked Mr. Capra whether it limited his film with General Patton directing the film.

"My boy, a director has the final cut on the editing floor."

Graham Martin took an invested interest in finding the African Mozart. Many important supporters joined knowing that he approved. Many, including a governor wrote in support, officially requesting assistance be given to me to on behalf of this mission of peace. I once asked Graham for a letter of support. I wished now I had pushed him a little harder. He responded to my request with an affirmative to write a letter. He followed this expressing a concern that his name might be controversial. He felt that a letter from him could prove detrimental. Feeling always intimidated and in awe of him in his presence, I said no more.

I knew that he wanted to see the film. His daughter told me that he had waited eagerly for my return from South Africa. His feelings had been hurt when I did not call immediately. My awe of him stopped me, hoping he would call me at his convenience and grant me a meeting. It was difficult believing that this great man waited for me.

Graham Martin died without seeing the film. I saw the New York Times photo of his burial in Washington, D.C., at Arlington National Cemetery. The obits, of course, centered on Vietnam. I hope this book sheds new light on a great American.

There are the straight forward parts to this story. There are the inexplicable parts. I wrestle with the straight forward parts. I could not have published a book at the time of these events without compromising lives. I believe enough time has passed. South Africa is a democracy with a government elected by a majority. Even so, there is a fear that I could betray confidences.

The inexplicable part of this story is easier to write. This part is off of the world's stage. Because the inexplicable in my life came from just this side of the extraordinary, each reckoning occurred with a connecting thread. It was as though there was a puppet master creating the drama.

I returned to the United States and my work as a composer. One of the first plays I worked on was "A Nightingale Sang". Set in World War II during the bombing raids, a blue collar English family struggles with relationships during the war. A daughter develops a relationship with a soldier. Walking with a limp, she has had no confidence with men. Meeting a soldier, a relationship develops outside of the family's knowledge. At a dance, the band plays "A Nightingale Sang in Berkeley Square."

A romantic moment during war performed in a theater, followed my return from South Africa. The music filled the dark theater. Memory flooded, and I returned to South Africa. The following months I returned again and again each time I sat at the piano and played the title song.

The longing was compounded by the fact that in the play the soldier returned home leaving the girl alone on a park bench. Who was this puppet master?

The intensity from memory increased after I composed an incidental score for Athol Fugard's Blood Knot.

It was the second call of the puppet master.

I set my course. I would return to South Africa. I would find support to make a documentary film. The African Mozart had to be there. If a conservatory of music could be built for housing the music of Africa, musicians trained, research encouraged, in a decade, there would be black classical musicians. I was confident I was right.

Christmas of 1987 I composed a score for Dickens' A Christmas Carol. With the fee I bought a plane ticket for a trip the month of February. I had no concrete plans. I notified no one I was coming. I followed my passion for Africa and prepared to return.

PART TWO

CHAPTER 10
Arrival Again

It was 8 a.m. The SAL plane descended over the Transvaal landing at Jan Smuts International. Two other Americans deplaned with me on their way to meet Francois Odendaal for another river expedition. Francois and his family had cleared a last minute visa for my trip. Francois had not heard from me. He did not know that I was on the plane with his associates. A small Volkswagen met us with our gear at the entrance to the airport. This included a large 12' canoe. The Volkswagen wore the canoe like a hat, bow to stern balanced in the middle, tied with rope. Four passengers and a canoe drove halfway between Pretoria and Johannesburg, and dropped me off at a shop. Francois' sister worked at the shop. She called Philip Hattingh to tell him that I was in South Africa. Philip spoke with me and informed me that he was on his way to pick me up.

Sun baked, with jet lag, I relived my former adventure through a mental fog. I had traveled eight hours from JFK to Frankfurt, Germany, a layover of six hours, then a flight to Johannesburg of 21 hours, with a stop in Windhoek, Namibia.

Greeting me were the then familiar breezes of the South African summer. Names returned from memory. Soon I could take up where former days left me painfully enchanted. The students at Teknikon, Fanie Van der Merve, beautiful Veronique. Africa's heart, Kathy Weir had mentioned marriage in a letter. Were she and Paul husband and wife?

The monstrous stone walls in Johannesburg reminded me of the South African Broadcasting Corporation, behind which was the orchestra and the impregnable State Theater in Pretoria. I had two weeks to get inside those walls.

Shortly after 3 p.m., Philip Hattingh walked into the shop. He greeted me warmly. There was no evidence that he thought I was the idiot I felt I was having arrived without telling anyone I was coming. With him was Reinhold Thaumuller. Reinhold was the head of the film unit for the South African Tourism Board where Philip worked as a film editor.

We went to an outdoor bar. Ordering beers, I filled them in on my developments. I had a letter from a PBS affiliate supporting my project. In the letter was a sentence stating any film made on my project would air on their station. This was a key sentence. The film unit of South African Tourism could gain points showing up with an American would could offer what they had been denied due to sanctions.

Suddenly I had assurances of meetings with influential people who could bypass the SABC. Reinhold cynically expressed his opinion that if I wanted something to fail, the SABC was the way to go.

This point I knew. After I had met with the South African Broadcast producers during my first visit and presented the concept that music could bring a message of conciliation, I was politely thanked for my heart felt interest in South Africa. Six months later back in the United States, Francois called me to tell me a news item in the Washington Post reported that the South African Government had spent half a million dollars on a We are the World-type song with images of happy times between races. It failed, and heads rolled at the SABC.

Philip extended his hospitality inviting me to stay at his house. I met Philip's wife, Wendy. She was a dancer, having studied at the Martha

Graham school in New York City. Eight years later, I toured as company pianist for the Asian tour of the Martha Graham Dance Company. More threads of the puppet master.

Over more beers, I played my score of Athol Fugard's Blood Knot for Reinhold, Philip, and Wendy.

Reinhold found the music humorous.

"That is Hollywood's view of Africa," he critiqued.

"You should do more research," he continued. "To the western ear, African music seems 'out of tune'. You need to listen until the African singing no longer sounds out of tune to your trained ears."

Philip and Wendy were tall, over six feet. She had the body of a Graham dancer, long line, muscular, dramatic. Philip,' a half-breed', as he called himself, part English, part Afrikaner, was soft spoken with a playful side that showed its colors with pranks at my expense.

These pranks included setting up a fake arrest, where a group of guys, one in a police uniform, would storm me, hand cuff me, and accuse me of breaking South African law. The day the prank was to take place, Philip thought better of it, filling me in, and asking me to act as if I didn't know. The policeman got cold feet so it was called off.

Weddings traditionally had this kind of hazing. The groom was loaded with alcohol, then when he passed out, his leg was put in a cast and he was driven miles from home waking in a distant train station.

Reinhold Thaumuller's family came to Southwest Africa from Germany. Southwest Africa became Namibia and many whites moved to South Africa following the transfer of power. While most of the film unit for SATOUR were suspicious of South African government policy, they worked for them and were paid by them to support a non political agenda, which turned any film into politics trying not to aspire to politics. I qualified for this political 'non- political' agenda.

Reinhold was average height, 5'9". Stocky without being overweight, bearded, like Fanie Van der Merve, he preferred the bush of the Kalahari to my concert halls. Once stranded in the desert, under a blistering heat, a film unit transport broken down, his crew spent the day under the van or "combi" low on water. Reinhold searched the area for a way to fix the combi. They had maybe one day before the desert heat threatened lives. Finding a heap of parts from a wrecked tractor, Reinhold looked for and found bolts he could substitute on the van. Rigging the van, he successfully repaired it, and returned to Pretoria.

During dinner plans were made. I would come with Philip to the office the next day. A meeting would be set with SATOUR officials. If one of them heard me doors would open. Reinhold was confident of this.

Over the next two years, Reinhold and I would act when others gave up. Our relationship, straightforward and mutually beneficial, would guarantee the completion of a film and its airing on television in the United States. The success would prove costly to both of us.

11p.m. I lay in bed. In the middle of the night I abruptly sat up awaking from a deep sleep. Disoriented, I did not recognize the room. I did not know where I was. My heart pounded. I awoke stranded in space. I was alone.

The next day I would meet the tiger on whose back I was to ride.

CHAPTER 11
The Meeting

Reinhold's film unit office was in Verwoerdburg, a section of Pretoria named after the father of apartheid, who was stabbed to death by a white disgruntled madman when the government was in session in the 1950's. The building's architecture was utilitarian surrounded by shops and parking lots baking in the summer's heat. Civilized Africa contrasts the bush or homelands with the dressing of western progress. While the bush breathed life, the city sucked it dry. Claustrophobia was what I felt whenever I spent hours in South African city malls and office spaces. I have never felt that way in New York City.

It was 10 a.m. when I arrived at the film unit. More beers were opened. Reinhold introduced me to his staff. His secretary, a woman in her mid life, was loquacious and always curious about the United States. Her daughter planned a trip within the year to the United States in order to visit a pen pal serving time in a penitentiary in Iowa. Patrick Swayze was in a Civil War epic running on South African television, and she wanted to know whether I knew him. She was a host for body building contests and had met and had photos taken with Arnold Schwarzenager when he visited South Africa as a competitive body builder.

Reinhold's assistant, Marlize, was 22 years old, blond, very attractive, shy and soft-spoken. She graciously assisted Reinhold to make me comfortable. There was, clearly, more than the formal relationship between them. I played the ignorant foreign gentleman, a role which earned me respect from Reinhold's secretary. She remarked how free of four letter words my vocabulary was in contrast to her boss and fellow film unit personnel. She figured this gentlemanly manner was due to the fact that I was originally from the American south, home of gentlemen aristocrats.

Pierre Van Heerden was present. I had met him my first trip. A cameraman, he had shot Amazon with Fanie for Francois. His wife was a seamstress for the theater, and had cut and sewn an African bush shirt and pants for me.

The back room was the editing room. Before digital editing, the editing room had a movieola for cutting rushes. It was a glorious machine. Two spools for film, two for sound mag tape, and a small screen where the editor could see the rushes. An editing room, when active, included sounds of a reel and mag tape screeching back and forward, snippets of sound, music, voice tracks, and a floor covered in cut film. The editor for a film was its true parent. Their power was supreme.

Before Amazon I knew nothing about film making. By the time I was being given the tour of the film unit of SATOUR, I had the trade speak in order. That being the case, no one there ever associated me with being a composer of classical music, nor did they care. Only one individual in South Africa would come to truly know me as a composer. He would become my greatest friend among Afrikaners, one who stood ground on my behalf during my darkest hour in South Africa. I would soon meet him.

The meeting that day at the film unit was with Gunther Detweiler in his office. Sitting behind his desk, he was stiff and nervous meeting me. An American was a serious liability. A relationship with me could jeopardize job security by making a reckless decision. I was nervous, so I muttered my usual incoherent presentation. It seemed, as the case had been with the SABC, I was to be thanked again for my heart felt interest in South Africa. Then the PBS affiliate letter, at Reinhold's suggestion, was placed in front of Gunther Detweiler. The sentence that guaranteed broadcast caught his eye. He looked up, and looked at me. "Perhaps you should speak with the chairman, Danie Hough, a very busy man, but there might be thirty minutes he could squeeze you in." Gunther Detweiler knew there was an opportunity, but he was not going to go out on an American limb for it. He gave me some time at the end of the week. This was problematic. I had only two weeks.

I thanked him. Another official entered the room. He introduced himself, Dale Pretorius. This was a famous last name in Afrikanerdom. A Pretorius had gathered a group of Afrikaners in Cape Town and made a trek to where the Zulus had slaughtered Afrikaner settlers. Fending off 10,000 war ready Zulu warriors, the band of three hundred Afrikaner men and women had claimed the day, dedicating the land to God, naming the river where bodies of Zulus turned it red, Blood River. The date in December was celebrated as the holiest of days. A giant museum sitting on a hill outside of Pretoria was the mecca of Afrikanerdom. Yearly treks were symbolically made from the Cape to Pretoria, reenacting the historic trek in covered wagons.

Dale Pretorius had worked in the New York City office and knew the American machine. He was far more comfortable with my presence, inviting me to join them for a drink in the executive suite. Business done, I was invited to relax with them.

Another official, Reg Swart joined us. He was in charge of SATOUR image making. This being the case he asked me what Americans thought of South Africa.

No longer under pressure, I relaxed and answered unguarded.

"Basically, Americans know little nor care. They are more interested in bargains at the store and whether taxes are taking away their bargaining power. South African news confuses many. Only a small percentage have any grasp of the South African conflict. This is divided into smaller groups, one pushing forward sanctions, the other feeling this is not the way to help. The vast majority dismiss the expression of an opinion with the excuse that they know little about that part of the world."

I continued. "There is a rich untapped culture in South Africa. South Africa can say more of herself developing her culture. African music, Afrikaner music, the fact that both have begun crossing over, reflects a multicultural future. Tell this story with music and young people dreaming , like the film Fame, and there would be interest from a majority of Americans. Find the African Mozart independent from government policy. Tell the story honestly. Otherwise, you will be creating propaganda." There was a moment of silence. I listened to the ice cubes clink in my glass. Gunther Detweiler finally spoke. There was emotion in his voice. He seemed on the verge of tears.

"It is a deep privilege to meet you, Patrick. These are words of a brave man who has a big heart. The Chairman must not meet you in a sterile office in order hear what we have heard." Nods of approval surrounded me. "I will ask the Chairman to meet with you in his home. With a more relaxed environment you can be comfortable, as you should be."

Philip Hattingh entered the room. He and Reinhold stiffened hearing the recent development. Two scotches later we called it a day.

What had occurred? Reinhold explained.

"If Gunther succeeds you will have dinner tomorrow evening with the number three man in the South African government. Danie Hough is not only head of SATOUR he is the governor of the Transvaal. If he approves your project, every door in South Africa will be opened to you."Reinhold spoke with nervous anticipation.

"You're either a bloody fool, or a fucking genius!"

CHAPTER 12
Johannesburg

I had to wait. Philip Hattingh drove me to Johannesburg. I wanted to find Kathy Weir and Paul Myburgh. I had agreed to tell my story to the heart of Afrikanerdom, hoping to be allowed to search for the African Mozart. Kathy's warnings about being wined and dined betrayed our trust, betrayed the magic that was Kathy's Africa.

Paul owned a Tangori Chicken place in Hillbrow. I found it easily, the entrance painted in bright yellows and reds, tables outside on the sidewalk. When I entered, Kathy Weir's mother Connie, looked surprised, but informed me that Kathy had stepped out and would soon return. I felt awkward waiting, the American bullying his way once again into their lives. Connie graciously invited me to come to their home that evening for dinner.

Waiting, I heard an American accent. He was thirty years old by estimate, and while cordial, seemed anxious. I introduced myself, and he invited me to join him. I asked the reason for his time in South Africa. He explained that he was there in order to complete a study on poverty in South Africa. He had been in South Africa a year and was eager to leave.

Didn't he find South Africa a place of magic?

"Yes. If you are white."

Kathy entered the shop and seeing me, stopped, took a second look, and in disbelief came up to me.

"What are you doing here?"

I had not said anything to the American. He waited to hear the answer, too.

My answer. Because I had promised I would return.

The American stood and left.

Connie then mentioned to Kathy that I would be joining them for dinner. Kathy was confused. It was a very awkward moment.

I rode to the Weir's home with Connie. Paul Myburgh would join us for dinner.

Connie and Dennis Weir were of Irish descent. They had always treated me with affection, extending hospitality whenever I was available. I carried intense guilt being in love their daughter. They either felt I was good for Kathy, or that she was old enough to live her own life.

I had the same guilt at the Weir home when Paul arrived.

"You silly American. You've come to help South Africa again?"

His face crinkled with laughter, a naughty laugh.

I nodded.

"Patrick is so polite."

Paul hated Americans, but loved their money. Otherwise, we raped the earth with our chemicals and opinions.

I needed to assuage my guilt. Once alone, I assured him that I had not had any sexual intimacy with Kathy.

Another naughty laugh.

"Of course you didn't. She was a virgin."

Paul Myburgh for seven years had lived, hunted, and become a family member of a Bushman tribe. He spoke the clicking language fluently. Burying film in the desert sand, once trusted, he documented life with these ancient indigenous peoples. He created a film, People of the Great Sand Face, and for his commitment, became a spokesman for the tragedy inflicted on indigenous peoples by modern man's progress. At his insistence, I had viewed the film. His fame and self assured manner kept me in awe. Kathy Weir, a recent graduate of the film school, and a serious talent according to Fanie Van der Merve, albeit reckless, came into Paul's life my first trip when we met him late the evening I spent with Kathy showing me her Africa. They were now lovers.

Paul's sand colored hair fell to his shoulders. Deep, piercing blue eyes sat in a round face that constantly studied the modus operandi of one's intent. In his childlike countenance there was a strength of a thousand year old myth.

Kathy Weir was untamable. She was a spirited wild one. In that she was totally a daughter of Paul Myburgh's Africa. Paul never wore shoes. He felt they were an anathema to walking on the earth. He walked, unhurried. Kathy leapt over sands and bush. They met when the sun went down over Johannesburg, the sunset Kathy loved.

I loved Kathy Weir. I had resisted American imperialist habits and left her a maid. I had showed up again not forgetting my feelings, feeling them yet more intensely, but remaining in a sense, hiding behind an African bush observing what belonged to two other people.

At dinner, I explained why I wanted to continue coming to South Africa. I shared the progress thus far and the possible meeting. I fully expected to be challenged. No one did so, in fact, Paul was more interested hearing the music I had brought, composed for Athol Fugard's Blood Knot.

I gave him the audio cassette copy. The Weir's, Kathy, and Paul listened quietly.

"Lovely."

Paul remarked that it was an honest representation of any indigenous music. It had the essence. He said nothing about my needing to learn to hear out of tune.

Kathy wanted to know whether this meeting would open up doors for my music to be performed by the orchestra. I hoped so.

Then it was the puppet master's turn. I can explain what followed in no other way.

Dennis Weir asked whether I would suffer him to play his kind of music. He went to get a 33 rpm record. Pulling it from the jacket, he placed it on the turn table.

After a four bar intro, the Weir's dining room flooded with enchantment. There it was. The song. A Nightingale Sang in Berkeley Square.

I sat at a piano and played this over and over for months. It kept me in its web remembering the night Kathy Weir took me to Johannesburg. It had little to do with finding an African Mozart, yet it was the melody that meant Kathy's Africa.

Dennis Weir had no idea what the song meant to me. Neither did Kathy or Paul. It had remained with me, a presence again thanks to the puppet master.

When I decided to write a book from the journal I kept the years in South Africa, the puppet master again threw this inexplicable web over my experience. I went to hear a friend of the family performing his cabaret show midtown Manhattan. At the restaurant, waiting to go to the back room for the show, I listened to a singer-pianist near the bar. As I passed him, he played a four bar intro and for the first time since that evening in 1988 at the Weir's home I heard..."that certain night, the night we met..."

CHAPTER 13
The Chairman

The following morning I returned to Pretoria. Philip Hattingh informed me that we would have dinner that evening at the chairman's home. There was a festive atmosphere at the film unit office. No one there had been invited before to the chairman's home. There was a subtle change in attitude towards me. I was a liability.

No one in the office regarded an African Mozart a raison d'etre. They were filmmakers. I could get their film to American viewers. Their film. It was far too early to absorb what the price would be. I was a composer looking for a remarkable talent in a place of war. Unless one lived in a township, there was no evidence of war. Business as usual.

Dinner was at 7. Three cars from the film unit left together for the drive to the chairman's neighborhood. It was located on the hillsides outside of Pretoria. Lush floral bush and gardens lined the well marked roads where quiet security belied any conflict. The evening sky gave a smooth even light to the homes of the privileged. Nature remained impartial.

We arrived. This was a beautiful residence. African art of a quality I had never seen filled the space with subtlety, not garish, but seductive. Otherwise, the polished floors, spotless glass sliding doors, and Park Avenue quality furnishing might as well have been wealth's norm.

I was introduced to the chairman.

"This is our honored guest!"

I was what?

Danie Hough was the administrator of the Transvaal. This included Pretoria, Johannesburg, extending through the high veld. He had been administrator of what had been Southwest Africa, now Namibia. He had gone lion hunting with Joseph Savimbi, Angolan president, a fact shared with me in confidence. Such a relationship was not publicly shared policy. There were a lot of quirky corners in African politics I daily became privy to. I share many of these without justification. They are a part of this story told with enough time having past. I hope that it will harm no friend in South Africa.

Danie Hough was about 6 feet 4 inches. Afrikaner men as a rule were above average in height. He was the Great White hunter stereotype. His voice had the timbre of a lion's. He was the classical movie image a boy like me grew up imagining; the hunter who tamed the "dark continent". I was appropriately intimidated.

"If he hears your story, every door in South Africa will be opened to you." Philip reminded me as we approached Danie Hough's home.

En mass we moved to the outdoor patio. This proved extraordinary. Elegantly set, an expansive table enough to seat twenty guests was prepared with place settings on white table cloth draping the table. Wine glasses, flowers, and softly lit lanterns added to the ambiance appropriate for state dinners.

I was introduced to the chairman's wife, a woman, who attractive and comfortable with her beauty, still had a large role to invent as wife of one of South Africa's powerful leaders. Afrikaner leaders I met always gave equal roles to their wives, whether the wife wished it or not. I often wondered whether this began during their days trekking from Cape Town. Women carried the same burdens in the bush, even during wars when they also handled rifles. This was true at Blood River, true during the Boer Wars. It is my assessment that I never saw a second class woman among the Afrikaners.

Past the patio was a pool. Further on in the darkness was a descending hill. In those shadows was African truth. There I lived in reverie. Somewhere out there was an African Mozart. Would Danie Hough hear my story?

At the table were other government officials, including Gunther Detweiler, who had arranged this dinner. The film unit was uncomfortable hovering at a far end of the table. They would take the fall if I proved a disaster.

Danie Hough sat at the head, placing me to his right. Directly across from me I was introduced to Schalk Visser, head of music for the State Theater, that impregnable fortress of art that had remained so to date.

His wife, Delene, sat to his left. She was twenty years his junior, very attractive, well spoken, and gracious to me. With the chairman listening, my first conversations were with Schalk Visser. Dinner served, my eating was limited since with Schalk I could discuss music. He was reserved in the first moments of our conversation. I shared with him my life as a composer in the United States, the subsequent journey to South Africa with a film score for an American film South African produced about a journey on the Amazon. I openly shared the thrill South Africa had created during my first visit, and the resulting dream of finding a musical talent that would change the classical history of music. I wanted to find that individual and return to the United States with the discovery.

Schalk explained to me that much was being done to secure a strong musical life in his programs at the State Theater, including sending out members of the South African Symphony to play educational programs in the townships. He expressed enthusiasm in the success thus far with developing opportunities for both black musicians and white. He said that due to the political differences, many blacks were not participating in fear of reprisals. Even so, he felt many were taking the opportunity. He offered to include me in the coming days traveling to the townships with the musicians.

The chairman listened and addressed me.

"Are you saying that South Africa is spending too much time and money on politics? Do I understand you correctly that the music Schalk's programs invests funds in has a longer lasting effect for South Africa?"

"It is your greatest treasure. Greater than your gold or your diamonds," I said. I have no idea where these words came from.

The chairman looked down the table at his guests.

"Our honored guest has brought us a gift. On behalf of South Africa, I thank you. You have spoken well. How may we assist you?"

I expressed the interest in seeing all the venues of music.

He gave instructions.

"Patrick is now an official guest of South Africa. Make arrangements for him for hotel. Schalk can show him his programs at the State Theater. We'll then fly him to Cape Town. Make arrangements for him there. When are you scheduled to leave South Africa?"

I answered that I had limited time.

"Reschedule his flight so that he can complete the agenda we arrange for him. We will pay for your visit as our guest."

It was a midsummer night's reverie. In those shadows past the pool's light I dreamed the rest of the evening. I dreamt that I was asked to play. Taking the music my hands had absorbed from Africa, for Schalk's benefit, I created a fugue. I was flying. The African night's fragrant air fulfilled a dream. A new classical music from the soil of Africa. "You have that," the chairman said.

Back home I would shake myself awake. I would look around the room, and settle that it was a lovely flight from reality.

The next morning awaking in bed at the Burgerspark Hotel I looked around the room. It had all happened. It was true. I yet lived in my improbable African story. For months there were only ghostly echoes of conversations and promises I had made deemed foolish and unrealistic by friend and family.

It was a dream and it wasn't.

CHAPTER 14
Schalk Visser

"Our ambassador in Washington had good things to say about you."
Schalk Visser met me in his office at the State Theater. I was surprised.
I had never spoken with the ambassador. It explained the reception
the night before as honored guest. Who and how had the ambassador
been supplied with any report? They were a cautious lot. I asked what
he had said. Schalk told me I was one of the most promising talents in
America. To date I have no clue where this assessment originated.

Schalk had his own questions. Why did Americans despise Afrikaners?

"The truth is few care," I told him. "South Africa is too far away. Our
own racial conflicts are easily transferred. Knowing little, Americans
buttonhole South Africa. Those who are knowledgeable feel hostile if
their politics are antigovernment, others tolerant if taking the view
that industry governs politics. In this sense, there is the same variety of
opinion in South Africa."

Learn our music... The black musicians' words and lives came to
light again. The American at Paul Myburgh's restaurant. South Africa
is magic 'if you are white'. Veronique's wall-filled photos of violence
in the townships. Decay hidden from sight, a reality I had not seen.
There was reason to hate the Afrikaner's blind cruelty. My day of
would come. Every revelation should have justified hatred, yet I never
hated. I still don't.

Schalk Visser's friendship based on the love of music remains the heart, ceasing judgment of South Africa. Music is not immune to man's cruelty to man, yet it is evidence of man's loftier hopes. Schalk lived this way, whether assessing him naive or not.

He was slight physically, in his 60's. He had a habit of pinching his face in conversation, with a well trimmed mustache could appear aloof or cold. In fact, he was vulnerable. His sensitivity made us quick friends.

Growing up on a farm in South Africa, he began music studies later in Europe, and returned to work for the Arts Council of the Transvaal. Originally located in Johannesburg, once the State Theater was built, he became head of music for the State Theater and the Transvaal.

I grew up near the horse farms in Kentucky's blue grass, beginning music with my mother. I had left home early to study music. Writing this book 8000 miles away from South Africa years have passed since Schalk and I first met. Distance and time diminishes fear. I remember now a rare friendship apart from the horrors that would come in the days following our introduction at the chairman's home.

Arrangements had been made for me to accompany a group of musicians from the National Symphony who were visiting schools as part of a music education program of Schalk's.

At an Afrikaner elementary school we were greeted by the principal. Shy yet hospitable, he offered coffee while students were brought to the auditorium. Two singers with an accompanist and I waited. Students entered quietly. There was no din of conversation. Order and respect for authority prevailed. I doubt there has ever been a more polite and eager to please society that created and held onto a system as evil as apartheid. How did it happen, I wondered that day.

Following the morning program, the accompanist, a pudgy faced man in his early 20's, told me about his music compositions sitting in a trunk unperformed. Had I any suggestions? Continue composing. It must be first a passion. He listened. It was not what he wanted to hear.

If he had a work that deserved international attention he would have to wait. I could not tell him. He was white and an Afrikaner. If he denied his own history, his own music would have to deny his history. He would still be held in suspicion. Perhaps forever. Until apartheid ended, he would be limited to his own society. I offered to look at his music. He went away after that day without contacting me.

Shoshanguve township was our next stop. After this experience I wished I had spoken to the accompanist. It was in Shoshanguve that I saw the untapped source of a powerful music lying in front of his pudgy face. The accompanist had eyes and ears looking to the Western tradition. He should have looked around him.

A wind quintet from the National Symphony took me with them to Shoshanguve. With them, an African drummer, and a black singer. These are the frolicking jokesters I know well in New York City. Bad musical jokes and cheap beer.

Their presentation proved this true.

My first introduction to township living. Unpaved roads, children in school uniform, the heat of the African sun and the wisp of wind that has an air for the lungs breathed by the first homo sapiens.

"This is a flute. If you can do this, you can play the flute."

Paul Bagshaw pulled a Lion beer bottle to his mouth and blew.

Joe Robinson, clarinetist interrupted.

"Who would want to do that when you can do this! I can speak Zulu."

Squeak, squeak, squeak. The students laughed.

"I can speak Afrikanse."

The squeak soured loud, brash, annoying.

"Or, I can speak English!"

The clarinet made fart noises.

Children screamed with laughter.

How much do the instruments cost children asked?

Paul Bagshaw said 3000 Rand. Barry, an American bassoonist replied 4000 Rand.

Joe Robinson held up his clarinet.

"Anyone want to buy? Cheap, real cheap. 300 Rand."

Following the program children were given an opportunity to try and play the instruments.

On our way to the next program in Shoshanguve Paul told me they had one problem with these presentations. They had no traditional music to play. Would I arrange some for them? Yes, if I had some tapes of the music as a reference. Joe had a cassette recorder with him. He would tape our next visit where a choir was to welcome us.

Arriving at a teacher training college I heard a choir in the distance. Walking towards the main auditorium I heard my first melodies of African song. It emerged out of shadows of the hillside at Danie Hough's home. The soil shook as we walked towards the building; Africa's oldest music, unwritten, passed by voice, parent to child.

Entering the auditorium 60 people sat on stage. Accessible harmonies, lilting melody, bodies swaying, feet punctuating rhythm in syncopation to the hymn they sang. A solo voice, a response from the choir. No instruments, only voice.

At that moment I entered African life. As though I was walking through an endless valley, there on stage was the road home. Ahead a snow capped mountain, then once over the mountain, the valley of apartheid, ahead in the distance beyond, a vista of running brooks, dotted forest, where these people and their music led to a long searched for paradise. The voices of their children's innocence waited for decades to have a hearing, a welcoming, a celebration promised by a music that built homes no tyranny could remove, songs building a nation that would save them. Song after song. I did not want it to end.

Paul, Simon, Barry, Joe and I were transfixed. For the drummer and singer this was home. Joe pushed the recording button on the tape recorder.

From this tape recording I would create the arrangements I was asked to make for the players with me that day. These songs, ill set to western wind instruments, would be the key to a discovery. In Soweto, because of this music, a stunning new music would be born. In time my first attempts would be a catalyst for the Soweto String Quartet. Through them the world would hear for the first time. They would travel the world with this African song.

Darker days lay ahead meantime. There would be a price.

CHAPTER 15
The Beginning

Danie Hough had instructed his office to make reservations for the Burgerspark Hotel in Pretoria. I spent my first days in there in 1986. Following the visits to the townships with the musicians from the State Theater, I returned to the Burgerspark, unpacked my bags, opened the window, and breathed the fragrances that were my first impressions. The thrill returned once again. I wanted to return to what had enchanted me those first days.

I walked to Teknikon. I passed the State Theater remembering it had been impregnable only days before. The sun was high, mid-afternoon, the breezes soft. Burning to a ruddy red, I bought a Boer hat with a Zebra stripe at the hotel. I might has well hung a sign around my neck, 'hick from the bush'. There was finger pointing and laughter. "Where's your rifle, mate?"

Arriving at Teknikon, there were no students waiting for public transport. The school was empty. Fanie Van der Merve had returned to his own film studio and resigned as director. He was somewhere off in the bush filming.

Only trails of ghosts remained in the quad and the classrooms.

I had in the early days been unnamed, moving enchanted among the unnamed then. Those days were sweeter. Two black laborers who made music in the evenings had insisted I learn their music. The early days I had been free to move wherever I wanted to go for the full measure of those days. Ignorant to the tyranny so many lived, my route was a circuitous one via days with Fanie, Kathy Weir's Africa, Veronique, and a class of challenging film students.

I found the classroom where I had lectured on music. On a bulletin board outside the classroom in the quad were pictures of students from the present. Frozen in the photos were young people laughing, confident their days were soon.

I had left a note on that same bulletin board in 1986 stating I would return. I had.

No one was there to welcome me. Time had not stood still for my note. Foolishly, I had believed that my return would be as full of life as the photos on the bulletin board.

My photo came to life! A sudden burst and the frame lived, picking up where I had left the students in 1986.

There they were! Kathy Weir returning a frisbee. Veronique pulling my focus with her volcano erupting from those fathomless glances. Students pushed me to answer what I was impotent to answer.

Not this time!

You see, I was now a guest of the tourism board.

Lights in the room flickered. A power surge?

The present returned briefly, and the room was emptied of ghosts.

The memory ignited. The class returned. I lectured once more.

Thank you for waiting these months. It has been a remarkable journey, one I thank you for inspiring. My advice concerning craft and commitment remains true. I am able now to lead you to real work and life rewarding commitment. There are stories around you of a people and a music. There are children living with hopes and dreams where there are no evident reasons for hope. They sing a music that is ageless, free, and promises the same to all. Help me find the African Mozart! The courage you will need on this quest will guarantee immunity from cheap western commercialism. There is a story for each of you. I know it now. You see, I have recently succeeded in....

The word succeeded echoed in the chamber of the empty classroom. The eager faces evaporated. I walked to the entrance of the classroom where on a brick I had signed my name. My name was still there. Reality silenced my lecture. The essence of my lecture lived in a brick on that wall.

I turned out the light and returned to the Burgerspark Hotel.

I was scheduled for a trip to Cape Town the following morning. Veronique! It was her family home. Haunted by the empty classroom at Teknikon I decided to call her.

With memory, the fear of her volcano created indecision, and I resisted calling her immediately. I had doubts now having faced the darker side of South Africa as a guest of the tourism board. To truly understand the music with what little I comprehended, I had to do so staying in a five star hotel.

Later in the evening I called her. Her voice was gentle. She was glad to hear my voice.

"I'm flying to Cape Town tomorrow."

So was she. She could meet me for breakfast the morning she arrived. Her voice trembled. "Lovely", she said.

The plane flew over Bloemfontein, the mecca of the Afrikaner. Serious flooding had ended a ten year drought. The turbulence was enough to rock the plane. The pilots in South Africa having flown bush planes kept the bumpy altitude while passengers chatted away lively and unconcerned. US commercial flights avoid these bumpy altitudes.

Flying over Table Mountain the plane landed in Cape Town. Nature carved a dignified giant out of stone, one that watched over two major oceans of the world. Walking out of the Karoo, ancient man must have marveled. This mountain was, and remains a great judge.

With the advent of sailors, first Portuguese, then Dutch and English, Table Mountain, like Jove, judged these tiny sea going vessels. Luckless sailors were crushed by the winds of the great southeaster. Thus the tale of the Flying Dutchman.

At the Cape Town tourism office I was given the phone to speak with a man, Cedric John Adamson. He ran a school for the Cape 'coloreds', peoples that included Malay descendants, an apartheid classification in a no mans land between whites and blacks.

"Another American. You've come to help us. I've heard it before. Empty promises in exchange for a lovely time and stories to take home for credits falsely taken."

I told him I was a composer. There was silence on the other end.

"We don't need our music stolen." He hung up on me.

I said nothing to the staff at the tourism office.

Two hours passed. Then the office started filling with men who arrived and said nothing. Their smoking filled the room with billows of smoke. One man had a banjo, another a trumpet, and a third a tuba.

The office door swung open. In walked a man who looked like a south sea island hotel owner. A round face, a thinly trimmed mustache, 6' 2" and dressed in white pants and jacket. He looked at me. I was sentenced.

He lectured me. I was condemned for my presumptuous behavior while the other men sat quietly in the room. The smoke gave the room an ambiance of Rick's in Casa Blanca.

"What sort of music do you write?"

I am a classical musician.

He became suddenly quiet. This made a difference?

"I apologize. You aren't what I thought you were. I brought these men with me to witness American theft. Your Paul Simon sits well in his penthouse suite. We will begin again. A classical musician has no such intention. What is your name? Come this evening to my home. We will have dinner and talk."

That evening at Cedric John Adamson's apartment he spoke at length until 3 am. He wanted me to know I would get little from tourism. There was a darker chapter to apartheid in Cape Town that tourism would not share with me.

"The government demolished District Six and wiped out the best homes of the old Malay quarter. There had been a wonderful night life in this quarter much like New Orleans in your country. There was crime, true, but there was also a vibrant creative life. That has now been erased and replaced with quiet neighborhoods for the whites. A mosque is all that remains of the old Malay quarter. You see it is against South African law to destroy religious buildings. But destroy a culture?"

Cedric John Adamson ran the oldest music training center in Cape Town for the 'coloreds'. Opera, musical, and street festival performers had gone on to perform with New York City opera companies. These singers were the first to have learned and performed opera in South Africa.

He showed me a video. Full costume, set, and well prepared, they sang Verdi's, La Traviatta.

"They don't read music, Patrick. I teach them through imitation and through listening to recordings. That rehearsal pianist you are seeing isn't reading music. He is playing by ear and from memory."

A three hour opera played by ear and memory?

"Don't forget us, Patrick. We need so much. A multicultural conservatory is my dream. There are things I cannot share with you since you are a guest of tourism. First, it would place your life in danger, and secondly, I would end up in prison on Robben Island where all of the leaders of the African National Party presently are. As long as you keep to music, you will be in the company of decent government officials. If you get nosy and it gets to another smaller group of officials, you will be a liability. I promise you, you don't want to meet these men. This conversation must remain here and not leave these doors. You are walking a line whether you knew it or not. You have a good heart and it serves you well. Otherwise I would have never invited you here."

I promised I would return with some fruit of our chat. At the very least with a way to get his message to a larger audience.

When I left at 3 am, I took with me a new fear. How could I have been so naive? They were watching me! Everything I said was being scrutinized. I knew now that I was a fool. Go home. Forget it.

I had heard music. Potent music. Music that inspired a passion greater than a peaceful life lived within the borders of my nation. There was a cost. Not just my life. Cedric John Adamson's trust affected me. Many opened their trust. For these reasons it was time to tell the story.

I decided I would film the people and the stories I had been privy to. I needed to go home and make plans.

The following morning I waited for Veronique. I would speak little of what I had heard the night before.

Sitting in the hotel lobby, I waited. I saw her enter and walk up to the reception desk. Wearing a summer cotton dress and a floppy hat she looked around the room and saw me waiting for her. I walked up to her and held her, her body comfortably reminding me of the tale of a lover's. I kissed her. She warmly smiled. Holding her hand we went to breakfast in the hotel restaurant. She had much to share.

"I left Pretoria. I felt harassed by the macho environment. Then I was hired by Canon Films and I felt harassed again. I've come home to study drama, and I am on my way this morning to sign up for classes. How are you? I have often thought of you. You do leave a lovely impression."

Her fire softened with these words. I told her about tourism and my plan to return and film what I had experienced.

"You're working with the government?"

I could say no more. I wanted to. I wanted to be her hero, but Cedric John Adamson's words returned, "I would end up in a prison." Veronique's new life required her to commit to a society that was a lie. My appearance in her life had given her hope. Working with the government, I was now working with the source of her lie. Without divulging more, and thus compromising her safety, I remained quiet. I had joined the enemy.

Reality tortured me. I should have quit. I should have loved her. The success I shared with Veronique meant no more to her than some paper weight on a pile of government papers.

I should have, instead, taken her hand and walked over Table Mountain into the Great Karoo. Trailing the desert wind I could find sanity through her beautiful madness. Instead, I yielded to her prison when in parting I casually kissed her hand telling her- no- *I insisted that she write to me.*

Write what? Lies?

The return flight to the US was a peaceful one with my Boer hat and its Zebra stripe.

CHAPTER 16
The Puppet Master

A human being sits down and tells a story. One listens. The moment passes. Time passes. Bits of the story remain until certain pieces of your own life connect to the tale. Is it now your story to continue? Most people regarding the practical reasons for continuing leave well enough alone. A few souls attempt a step or two towards the wisp of an idea. Meeting resistance mostly in the form of criticism, their actions die in the wake of self doubt.

A few move on to the fool's road, so named by the graveyard of shipwrecks where luckless adventurers have failed. The wise wag a finger at the pipe dreamer. Known only to the adventurer is the puppet master, a presence, like the wind, going where it lists. The Great Story Maker. Destiny's master craftsman.

Only the handful who have stayed the course, stayed past the practical, past the criticism- only these find the wind. Fewer reap earthly rewards or fame unless they journey to the South Pole and return alive. Even then there are suspicions due to the fact that a story must be told and then believed. The story has to be listened to and listeners have to decide whether pieces of it connect to their lives. Few follow suit.

The puppet master is an impartial listener. His spirit leads the adventurer. A matter of choice. Listen, let it pass, or act?

Paul Myburgh told a story of the Bushman healing man. For the duration of dusk to dawn the healing man danced and sang. When there was the first light of dawn, the healing man experienced 'the little death' when healing administered new health for a people who had no contact with modern medicine.

An English anthropologist had accompanied Paul Myburgh on a trip through the Kalahari to visit the People of the Great Sand Face. A three day car ride, and a five day walk in the merciless Kalahari- the regular journey to the Bushmen. The Englishman suffered headaches walking in the desert. He assumed it was from the intensity of the desert sun.

Arriving at the village of the Bushmen, the healing man at dusk sang and danced. At first light he walked up to the Englishman, placed his mouth on the top of the Englishman's head, and sucked out tiny pieces of glass. The headaches abated.

A year prior to this, the Englishman had been in a car accident. His head had gone through the windshield. The healing man removed the remaining fragments of glass. How did he know? The healing man had never heard of automobiles.

Reinhold Thaumuller told the story of a young Zulu who worked for the film unit. On a film shoot the young man had gone into a state of shock . His face distorted, his eyes rolled backwards, and he shook. He was taken to the hospital. The family of the Zulu begged the hospital to allow them to take him to the sangoma, the medicine man of the Abantu speaking peoples. This was out of the question. For three days the youth lay in a hospital bed staring blankly into space. Finally, the doctors released him to his family. Two days later he returned to work. His family had taken him to the sangoma.

I often told my children stories. One concerned the puppet master.

"Who is stronger? You or the wind?"

"The wind," they answered. "That's easy!"

"Yes, the wind can lift that tree from its roots. It cannot, however, pull those little blades of grass from the ground. You can."

They picked the grass and held the blades to me. They acted on a story.

While I was in South Africa a tornado struck leaving devastation that made international news. My children were in its midst.

The puppet master made their story as he made mine. A story is told and hopefully, someone listens and acts.

I arrived in South Africa the third time a dashing successful adventurer. I had glowing recommendations from the United States, money for a film and a title, African Adagio. The optimistic Italian word, adagio, means "at rest". It was a double entendre for music and politics. I was prepared to be a bridge builder. There were no loose ends.

Friends would arrive in my imagination at Jan Smuts International and greet their hero. The choir from Shoshanguve would greet me with song and dance. I would walk into the terminal with a heightened sense of unity and purpose, decorated with sun glasses carefully placed, a choreographed walk anticipating the high drama that would overwhelm our first moments.

So much for cinematic images.

Rennie Clarke and Philip Hattingh met me at the airport with what would be hours of complaints about the film, money, and Reinhold Thaumuller. Outside the airport were the familiar hills of the Transvaal, the warm sun, the African clouds and wind that greeted me as an old friend.

"Patrick, there is no way this film can be done on the present budget. Reinhold has thrown this in my lap. I have to put aside other work and do this gratis. I'm putting you up in my house and there is nothing in the budget for these expenses."

I felt bodily exhaustion while I settled into the South African landscape.

Rennie Clarke's home was palatial. High ceilings were thatched with roofing styled after a Zulu kraal. There was a garden, a gardener, a maid, two automobiles. The home reflected the lifestyle of South Africa's rich and famous, liberal and eager to share with the black majority.

Rennie prided himself a liberal. He expressed his politics through cynical humor where nothing was sacred. Eliminate racial barriers through crudeness for all. No exceptions. Jews, ovens, blacks, tire necklaces, young women and sex, all aspects for which he believed an enlightened existentialist sneered.

He spoke like an M1 rifle firing at close range. Long discourses were followed with, "yeah? yeah?" making sure you were agreeing. He paused, waiting to hit the bull's eye. He often missed but did not have the humanity to see that he did.

He sat at his desk and mapped out African Adagio. None of it made sense. There were diagrams, scenic shots broken down, and arrows pointing to the ends of the diagram. Each pencil mark had with it a lengthy discourse and a philosophical sub text.

I endured his diatribe until the first meeting with Reinhold. Rennie talked as though this was a feature film shoot; booze, sex, drugs, and rock and roll. He insisted he knew how to make a film targeted for American television. the only one who knew how to shoot a great film.

Rennie Clarke was a noisy anachronism held over from the 60's. Creating a good film was a piece of cake. Those who were brilliant movers and shakers in the world ruled and took whatever they wanted.

If I supported him, I would join the pantheon of innovators. All that was required was for me to release control of the film to him.

I held the check, and Reinhold had control of the remainder of money for the film.

I returned to the country that had given me a story. Rennie Clarke strapped me to a seat for an intense survival course. Trust and friendship shifted to strategy, suspicion, and distrust.

Dark days arrived. I had been called friend until there was issue of control. Battle ready experiences teamed up to defeat former patterns of trust. I was alone. The meeting with Reinhold would confirm how alone I was.

The film unit office for tourism on Atterbury Road mixed suburban houses and business office complexes. The office was a three story unit, box like and functional. The view outside the windows welcomed the African sky, a friendly blue, the midday sun dancing on abundant plant and floral life in full bloom.

My old friends at the film unit were blowing their egos around. They spoke of the reason they were barking.

"Tourism heads know nothing about this film," Reinhold said.

Philip Hattingh and Rennie Clarke were present. Rennie interrupted.

"Look. We know how to make films, you don't. You were brought over to be the presenter for the film, period. We will make you a good picture, so relax."

Was it my story?

"This film must be centered around building a conservatory in order for a new classical music to emerge and a new music developed," I reminded them.

"No, it's not," Rennie snapped. "It's about South African music. Your friend Schalk Visser is an ass. So is Danie Hough. They are government mentality. If it is up to Schalk Visser this film will be about the State Theater."

Philip jumped in with a calmer view.

"You and I have been friends for a long time, yes? All of us are giving you our time gratis and believe in this film. We know better what is here in South Africa."

I was short.

"Yes, Philip. What is not being taken into consideration is that I raised money, American dollars, and I bought my own plane ticket when it was originally agreed you would do so, and I have nothing in a budget for a salary, too. If there is sacrifice here..."

Rennie interrupted.

"That's your problem. We are making a film that is considerably under budget with limited time to make it because we have real jobs here and you don't."

Reinhold placated.

"I was really pissed off that tourism promised you carte blanche in February, and gave you jack. I went to a contact in Foreign Affairs. He is risking his own career with this film. All we have to do is get this film aired in the States. Once it is flighted, he committed to other films for whatever budget we need. This film is a teaser."

Again Rennie broke in.

"This means Reinhold is the producer, I direct, Philip edits, and Reinhold and Pierre shoot."

I contested.

"I believe if you raise money you are a producer..."

Rennie shot back.

"Garbage! You are the presenter. Period."

I had met Rennie Clarke in 1988 at the tourism office when I was guest of tourism. He was a writer for their films. He had a goatee, long hair and had a ring in his ear. He was tall and thin. He claimed that he came from a wealthy whiskey making family in Scotland, had lived and taught in the United States at SUNY Purchase, had represented rock groups, and then moved to South Africa as a marketing strategist. He fit the Rolling Stones rock persona.

He ranted.

"I don't need your little film for my career. I need you to get it right. This film is an Indaba. It's Zulu for meeting place. It's Indaba not that ridiculously inflated title you want."

The Indaba ended on shaky grounds. Rennie suggested he meet with Schalk Visser at the State Theater to determine whether he would use anything for the film Indaba.

"Patrick will not have any time for social events until this film is shot. That will be in a week and a half."

Schalk Visser was shocked. He was taken aback by Rennie Clarke. Technical crew, schedules, and shoots were coldly discussed. The following night there was to be a performance at the State Theater of two pop stars of Afrikaner music. One artist was being flown from Cape Town for the film. After the disturbing meeting with Schalk, Rennie spent two more hours on the story board. It remained a maze of lines and an encyclopedia of anarchist philosophy.

The evening of the first film shoot I arrived early and introduced myself to one of the performers. Rennie arrived witnessing the exchange.

"Well, it appears you have everything under control. You direct!"

Rennie exited walking with directorial command, a cloud of smoke trailing his cigarette.

Pierre Van Heerden arrived filling in for Reinhold, who had another commitment.

"What am I shooting? Where is Rennie?" I filled Pierre in on Schalk's meeting.

"There are two singers, Pierre. Peter Westhuizen and Anna Lee Van Rouyen. I have met both. The plan is to record about three minutes of performance and then interview them. What is the shooting ratio?"

"One to one," Pierre laughed.

"In that case, I'll make sure my questions at the interview are economical."

"I want to shoot some cutaways," Pierre continued.

"Shooting an audience breaks the fourth wall. With Afrikaner music and an Afrikaner audience, breaking the fourth wall will make it political, don't you think? Viewers must hear music not wonder about a white audience."

The hall had been set up with tables for food, drink with candlelight.

"Those candles will make it difficult to see who is in the audience," Pierre contested.

We prepared to interview Peter Van Westhuizen in his dressing room. Rennie was still ranting in the hallway.

"I don't bloody care! This is bloody shit, shit music from a Cape coon, and a fucking Yank! They are all jerks!"

Apartheid classified Peter Westhuizen "colored" or "mixed race". Part Afrikaner, part African, he had risen in the society playing his own style of Afrikaner music. The political side made him nervous. He requested I stay away from this subject. He shared his story.

"I went to Cape Town from Namaaqualand when I was playing a three string guitar. I became fascinated with what music I heard from the six string guitar. I brought music that people play on the farm, and I first played like this."

He played. A jaunty folk strum. He continued.

"Then I heard people play this style."

It was a sophisticated jazz style with subtle bass lines and chords built with flat 9ths and 13ths. I remembered Cedric John Adamson's story of Traviatta learned by imitation.

I thanked him and invited him to come to the United States. It was a dream of his.

In the hall Rennie's anger at me fumed unabated.

"I quit! Reinhold can get another lackey to direct. I'm through with this American prick!"

Pierre moved the camera to the hall. There was a deafening ovation. Anna Lee Van Rouyen entered the stage. There was an obvious similarity to the Grand Ole Opry in Nashville performances and audiences.

Her music blended a Jacques Brel melody with an indigenous African rhythm. The mood shifted to a ballad.

Her audience quieted. The audience knew the words I didn't understand, and her melody took them to memories the Afrikaner language owned. In front of me a young couple leaned their heads together, taking hands.

We moved again to the dressing room following her performance. Anna Lee Van Rouyen was even more nervous than Peter Van Westhuizen. The dangerous American syndrome.

"Your audience loved you, Ms. Van Rouyen."

She had a singer's eyes, expressive, lit with a light when she performed. She was in her twenties.

"The Afrikaner is isolated by distance and now by sanctions. Here within your people's boundaries, your music reminded them, in my observation, of something they know and fondly remember. They responded to you with an ovation. Yet, because of sanctions, much of the West has negative impressions of the Afrikaner. If you played for an audience in New York, could you share your music with an audience greeting you with suspicion?"

She was uncomfortable with my question and began with a safe answer.

"I think music is a universal language..."

I pushed the issue.

"But there is universal distrust. Your art is hidden because of your language. The secrets of the Afrikaner folk history remain hidden from other cultures. The Afrikaner resolves this by giving only what he or she thinks the West wants to hear. I heard rhythms from indigenous African music in your songs, rhythms from a people who want equal voice, a voice your music makes equal."

Her showmanship vanished. Her eyes hardened. There was silence. Then she answered directly.

"The black is in our music. You are correct. After all, we grew up together on the farms. We are all Africa. We are the rhythms of Africa, those people are a part of us, and have affected us. Most Afrikaners are only now becoming aware of this. It has always been there, but we have denied it. Our language is full of African native words, our lives are mingled with their stories. It is within South Africa that music is universal, and it is there that we are writing a new history."

I smiled. She calmed, and returned a smile. I thanked her, and assured her that her music confirmed her candid answer.

I finally met Rennie in the hall.

"You wasted footage we don't have to waste. This dressing room is the pits. I would have shot you in the snack bar and then walking down the hall."

"You walked out, Rennie, and informed me I was directing, bothering not to ask what I was doing," I contested.

"You were to do nothing until I arrived."

"I was exploring material I would gladly have passed to you. I had no intention of directing," I offered.

"In that case, from now on I pick what to shoot, and you follow orders. I'm canceling this State Theater crap. I'll thank your friend, Schalk Visser, and dump his schedule. This crew needs to unwind from this debacle. I'm taking money from the budget to eat and feed them. They are owed it."

Cast and crew went to an Italian restaurant. 140 Rands were spent. I was treated with polite disdain.

Something had been said about me. It was clear that whatever it was, it would clinch final control to the Indaba film crew.

"I could not fathom you had said it," Reinhold lectured me.

The following day at Rennie Clarke's home, Reinhold Thaumuller, Philip Hattingh, and Pierre van Heerden came to confront me. Reinhold continued.

"Patrick said what?"

Pierre jumped in.

"Patrick said that I should shoot an all white audience."

Pierre had told everyone at the Italian restaurant the previous evening, everyone except me.

Earlier that morning I had asked Rennie to move me to Johannesburg. He had stalled until 3 pm when this bomb was dropped. These were the words that once passed to government watch dogs would place me in danger.

"This has been a dismal failure in communication thus far," I retorted helplessly. "Why would I have said this? I'm packing and going home. I'll present a story of dismal political failure attempting to make a film about a multiracial conservatory in South Africa. It's the usual fare being presented."

I played my trump card. They knew it was a death sentence relating this failure to the authorities. They would be held accountable for trusting me in the first place. A line was drawn. Reinhold took up the ball.

"I told them we must first speak to you, Patrick. I don't believe you said it. It points to the fact that none of us are clear about this film's theme. After a week of planning, we still do not have a story board."

Rennie made his entree.

"Your brain is mushy. We can't shoot a film until you clean up your act. Schalk Visser arranges something, we don't know why you want it, other than that he is your friend. There is not enough money for friendships. We know who needs to be in this film, and we know what Americans will want to see. I taught in the States, and I do know they don't want the shit you filmed last night!"

Reinhold offered a solution.

"We are going to isolate you for two days and allow you to get a clearer picture. There is a villa where I can make a reservation. We will cancel Schalk Visser's other groups for this weekend. I will politely thank him for you. Tuesday we will get together and set a schedule for a first rate film. Now that I have spoken with you I feel better. Let's seal this resolution with a braaivleis at my home tonight."

I did not want to be isolated by Indaba.

"Reinhold, I prefer to check into a hotel in Jo'burg. The city is emptying for Easter holiday and it will be quiet."

"No. We don't think you should have any distractions," Rennie bullied once again.

"I work better in a city. I sleep in villas." I responded.

Reinhold yielded. He would drive me to Johannesburg.

At the Holiday Inn on Empire Road in Johannesburg, Reinhold dropped me off. He shook my hand and told me he would see me in a few days.

There were people I needed to see.

CHAPTER 17
Jo'burg and Melville

Francois Odendaal had given me the name and phone number of an old friend living in Johannesburg who was a lawyer. He thought I might one day need her assistance. I called her and introduced myself. Her name was Anna Marie Englebrecht. I told her I was making a film and that I was in a big mess. She was happy to pick me up for dinner at her house that evening at 6. It was early afternoon.

Melville, the section of Johannesburg where Paul Myburgh lived, was walking distance from the Holiday Inn on Empire Road. It took me 20 minutes to walk. I found no one home. I left a note telling Paul I would be at Anna Marie Englebrecht's home that evening and left her phone number.

Melville was Johannesburg's artist colony. I ordered a late lunch at a Polynesian restaurant. At a table near me, a beautiful woman sat with a bespectacled man my age. Both were black. I introduced myself.

His name was Sipholu Raolo. He was a South African journalist who worked for CBS in South Africa. The woman was a model, having worked in Los Angeles before returning to South Africa.

Another associate of mine had made contacts with Mimi Edmonds, a producer for 60 Minutes, someone to call if I was in trouble. I asked whether he knew her. Yes, very well, he answered.

"My associate had attended Vassar with her twin sister," I said. He gave me his phone number and suggested we stay in touch.

At Anna Marie's home I was introduced to her brother, Johann, a flight attendant for the South African Airways leg to New York City. Anna Marie was usually in Namibia acting as legal counsel for the U.N. during the transition to independence. I was fortunate to find both at home. Johann had tough advice for me.

"Your mistake was getting involved in the first place with Pretoria. I think you should pack your bags and go home. This country will never change. They simply put on another face in order to maintain power. The men you are working with are in a habit of brow beating in order to manipulate. They aren't going to change because you have a dreamer's view of this country. They will simply use you. Forget them understanding your idea about an African Mozart and a conservatory."

Anna Marie was less reactionary, albeit Johann was right.

"I have some people here at the university who can help you research this idea. I am sure they will be both interested and helpful. I will also check on the legal aspects of breaking a contract. I advise you to find an excuse for staying in Jo'burg. Unless someone at the top in Pretoria exonerates you, you could be in danger."

I mentioned the letters of support I had from the United States. Johann warned me.

"You are in South Africa. Nothing will help you once you are a liability. Get the hell out of here before it is too late."

Dinner quieted our conversations to Johann's love of New York City, musicals, his extensive collection of recordings of musicals. Anna Marie spoke of her early days roaming the outback with Francois and his penchant for trouble. She felt he had a guardian angel watching him since he had survived so many close calls with death.

"Now I have a friend of his in the same boat," she said. "Let's hope you have his guardian angel."

Her phone rang. It was Paul Myburgh. I took the phone. He was laughing.

"You silly American. So, you finally came to help South Africa and you are in an even bigger mess. I'll come over and slap you to your senses."

When he arrived, Kathy Weir was with him. She chided me.

"Why did you contract with those people, Paddy? I warned you many times they would be trouble."

I filled them in on the film progress.

"You can't make a film on that budget," Paul reprimanded. "They are correct. They must have money from another source. As usual, you are stupid. For now that is not important. First, Kathy and I welcome you as an old friend. We must smoke the peace pipe."

I had been puffing on my pipe. I passed it to them.

Paul took a long draw.

"Don't you ever clean this thing?"

It was decided that I must remain in Johannesburg. Anna Marie offered me her home. I would have it to myself with Johann in flight and because of her trips to Namibia. Paul suggested I come to his Tangori Chicken restaurant the next day and discuss alternatives.

I awoke in the middle of the night tense with nausea. I threw up violently, the muscles in my body contracting painfully. In the morning, I showered and ate a light breakfast with Anna Marie and Johann saying nothing about the nausea.

Walking to Hillbrow, I passed through Wittswatersrand University. Students sat leisurely in the large open spaces near the commissary. They were like students everywhere. This university was known for its criticism of apartheid. Two weeks earlier, a professor known for open criticism of government policy had been assassinated on university grounds.

Would violence escalate? Civil war would empty these facilities leaving books scattered, with trash strewn on floors, steps, and balconies.

At Paul's restaurant, we looked closely at the mess I was in.

"The South African black has lost patience," Paul explained. "Revolution is months away. Hillbrow is a section of Jo'burg under

Separate Acts. Blacks are openly defying the government and moving here. Crime has increased dramatically. This time bomb ticks daily. America's involvement with their ridiculous grasp of this conflict is superfluous. They make not one iota of difference. If there is a revolution, America will do what it always does and run. It will be our destiny, one we must face. Tourism will never understand your classical music idea. Frankly, it is not clear to me. I, at least, hear your spirit, whether I understand it or not. Their films never have to sell in the market, and they reflect this. I am willing to make your film. I never have had problems selling my films. I will finish this for you so that you can stop coming back looking for something only you understand."

I agreed and accepted his offer. Paul and Kathy drove me back in his Mercedes an older model with doors I was chastised for slamming. At the Holiday Inn we drank beers and celebrated the new film. A waiter came to the table and told me I had a phone call.

It was Schalk Visser. He was upset, and had been trying to find me all day.

"We waited for you, Patrick. The choir singing traditional music arrived dressed and prepared. No one showed."

Clearly, Reinhold had not called Schalk to thank him and cancel the scheduled shoots.

I told him I would get back to him.

Returning to the table, I informed Paul and Kathy of this news. I requested some time in order to find out what had happened. I promised to get back to them and continue working on our film.

I had just tasted freedom from Indaba.

CHAPTER 18
The Indaba

9 o'clock that evening Schalk called me on the phone in my room at the Holiday Inn.

I informed him of the mess I was in.

"Schalk, I am very sorry. They told me the State Theater was crap, and ordered me to go off and think, telling me they were canceling anything you scheduled. I am speaking to another filmmaker in order to resume filming what I planned from my visit last time."

"Musicians at the jazz club as well as a choir were prepared for the filming," he responded.

"This is not good news. Was this the doings of Mr. Clarke? I find him an offensive individual. He should not be associated with your film."

I dropped the bomb.

"It has, unfortunately, taken a political turn. I have been accused of wanting to film a white audience for political reasons. One cameraman's word against mine. I am living with crippling fear that there is a plot and my life is in danger."

"Nonsense," Schalk curtly responded on the phone. "Your life is not in danger. This has become an ugly affair. Please don't leave South Africa. Let me see what I can do."

This mess would now go to the top. Schalk would have to defend me against a mob. It would be a long night.

I sat down and mentally erased Rennie Clarke's story board. The remainder of the evening I created one for African Adagio. When I finished, I had one hour to sleep before breakfast and the outcome of Indaba.

Reinhold was the first to call. He wasn't aggressive. He was frightened.

"My job is on the line and my contact in Foreign Affairs is about to get a hand slapping. How the hell did Schalk Visser get involved?"

I reminded him that he was to cancel scheduled shoots with Schalk and had not. Schalk had found me, and I had apologized. The white audience issue was moot at that point.

"Well, I'll be lucky if I have a job after this meeting."

He picked me up and drove to the tourism headquarters in Pretoria. Danie Hough had arranged a meeting with an official, Graham Smith. Reinhold and I entered his office. We sat across from him like two boys sent to the principal's office.

"Mr. Byers, I am Graham Smith. The Chairman, Danie Hough, asked me to meet with you in order to discuss your film and explore what we might do to assist you."

He offered coffee, and sent his secretary to bring it. He continued.

"The Chairman has instructed me to see whether we might make an acceptable agreement so that you may finish your film. I understand there are artistic disagreements presently relating to subject matter. While we cannot offer additional money, we can place our offices at your disposal with film equipment, transport within South Africa, and scheduling assistance. Under these conditions can you complete your film?"

I explained what I had intended to film from my former visit. I believed it would be a subject matter that built bridges between parties in conflict in South Africa. I had no intention of polarizing any one view against the other, and had been counseled by Americans with extensive experience in diplomacy before committing to the making of this film. I did not intend to make a film about South African stars in music. It was a film about dreams. Afrikaner dreams, Zulu dreams, Xhosa dreams, Malay dreams, and the stories passed down in their traditional music. "Find a Mozart to create music and South Africa could share who she truly is," I said.

He smiled an officious smile.

"Can we create one sentence out of these words as an agreement? I apologize for the need. It will clarify the goal and limit future misunderstandings. As a gesture of your friendship we would like to use footage in the future. We will offer no pressure, and do will so with your full knowledge of its use."

I accepted. With Reinhold there, I had another request.

"I would prefer to make this film without the participation of Rennie Clarke."

"You and Reinhold Thaumuller planned this film, thus you are co-producers and co-directors. It is your film to determine the direction and content together."

The meeting ended. Indaba was replaced. African Adagio would be made. I had mixed feelings. The working relationships would be at the very least functional. Paul Myburgh and Kathy Weir would consider me an idiot. Driving to the film unit I spoke to Reinhold.

"Let's make a simple film and stay away from 'stars'."

"I am in total agreement," he gave as a muted response. " Let's meet to make a schedule."

I told him I had a story board.

"Is that what you wanted?"

"It's fine. Could you at least speak to Rennie? I must work with these people everyday. It would be helpful to me," Reinhold pleaded.

At the film unit Rennie kept avoiding me. Chasing him, I cornered him. I asked if we could chat.

"I don't want to have anything to do with you," he snapped without making eye contact.

I phoned Schalk. He was elated.

"Come have dinner at my home this evening and we will celebrate. Later we can attend a performance of Lohengrin at the State Theater."

Indaba went out of the door with Rennie Clarke and his Scottish throne. The search for simpler dreams was in a new soil. African music sat on terra firma once again.

CHAPTER 19
Perestroika

At dinner that the evening in Schalk Visser's elegant home, I once again met Delene, his wife. She was a professor of math, another lovely, self-sufficient Afrikaner woman some years Schalk's junior. Their home sat at the top of a hill accessible by a winding drive. It overlooked other hills where other homes sat hidden in African flora. There was a pool elevated above the distant view of hills. Often in days to come, Schalk and I would swim in his pool. We both had a mutual love of wine. With a glass, we would listen to Mahler while military transport planes buzzed overhead.

The film shoot was scheduled to begin that week. I had the wind quintet arrangements that I had made from the indigenous choral music taped on my visit to Shoshanguve. The classical musicians were to meet with me prior to taking the arrangements to the townships. Schalk had scheduled filming youth from the Indian community who were studying Indian classical dance. There was a choir at the teachers college in the township of Shoshanguve, and then the journey to Cape Town for the Malay culture.

Soon Deklerk would be president, replacing Botha. Schalk felt confident it would be for the better. He often was a guest at the homes of these leaders. This was the first time I first heard from Schalk that once DeKlerk was president, Nelson Mandela would be released from prison. I kept it to myself. His trust and friendship I valued, thus never divulging this remarkable news upon my return to the United States. Six months following my return, Mr. Mandela was released.

The Indaba crew threw accusations of treasonous political intent concerning me at Danie Hough's home the night of my trial in abstencia. Schalk, alone, refuted each accusation, one by one. Schalk told me that my accusers had interrupted a birthday party, and Danie Hough was incensed.

Schalk's trust extended to including me in a state dinner shrouded in secrecy. The Soviet Union had never been allowed entree into South Africa. Soviet journalists worked every other desk in other African nations. Perestroika was altering the relationship, and the first Soviet journalists allowed to enter South Africa were being hosted with a dinner and a ballet, Prokofiev's Romeo and Juliet, at the State Theater.

There were three journalists at dinner. I was introduced. The 'american' part raised eyebrows. Foreign Affairs officials were the official hosts. The scenario speaks for itself. The journalist sitting directly across from me opened up in time. He was my age.

I asked him what he had experienced during the Cuban missile crisis when both of us were 14. His answer was curt.

"Nothing!" he snapped.

An insult. I thought so. He read my face. Then, reconsidering, he answered.

"We knew nothing. We were told nothing. If there was a war, it would have been a surprise to us," he said.

We attended the ballet, and I sat next to him. I spoke about classical music, my reason for being in South Africa, and what I hoped I would find. His English was limited, but he did speak it.

"I am surprised at the wealth of culture in South Africa. No other African nation I have reported on equals South Africa. This theater is equal to any in Moscow. I hope I can one day return. Good luck with your film and the African Mozart."

As he left for their hotel following the performance of Romeo and Juliet we shook hands outside of the theater. Crossing the street he turned and gave me the "peace" sign, laughing.

"Just think," Schalk remarked, "you are the only westerner to witness this moment. They were surprised to see a ballet with music by one of the great Russian composers played so well."

I mentioned the journalist had said as much.

Meanwhile, challenging days were ahead. There was little trust. I was crumbling physically and emotionally.

You must learn our music...wait until you see the sun setting over Johannesburg...failure is an orphan...

An African Mozart. It was quickly becoming preposterous.

CHAPTER 20
The Opening

"This is the bush veld in southern Africa where early man heard these sounds for the first time...."

On the 15th take, the opening remarks finally satisfied Reinhold. By then I was a ripe red appearing as though I had been under the bush sun for a week. It had, in fact, been only since 9 am that morning. It was 11 am.

Later, Paul Myburgh and I sat and improvised on thumb pianos while he spoke of the bushmen ,"when sound turned to music". Paul had agreed to participate.

Those were the days of 16 mm, labs, shooting ratios, and movieolas. 15 takes cost. It was a one or two take reality. Without any evidence of an African Mozart, this theme was understood by me alone.

Thus, African Adagio took peculiar turns in the road while shooting 'music'. Even Indaba found its way back onto the map. Zulu rock music, Sangoma 'witch doctor' dance and music, Boer traditional music were all shot in the Jo'burg-Pretoria area. The film crew, lackluster in attitude, barely spoke to me.

Two important shoots were scheduled at my request-- a meeting with the classical musicians from the National Orchestra with a choir in Shoshanguve in order to try my arrangements of traditional song, and a trip to Cape Town in order to speak with Cedric John Adamson. He, after all, understood an African Mozart.

At the end of each day I returned to Johann and Anna Marie Englebrecht's. Their housekeeper, Angelina, daily greeted me warmly. As many Africans did, she spoke Afrikanse and no English. She insisted I try to speak Afrikanse. Johann and Anna Marie were off elsewhere. I sat with my story board each evening looking at what had been shot and what I had written. I made notes. Often I looked off into space while one of Johann's opera recordings played.

Paul Myburgh had remarked that there was strength in being alone. It was a mantra out of my grasp. Numbing fear remained. When I was alone, the idea of an African classical orchestra and a music grew paper thin. Without substance, Kathy's African sun painfully ignored African Adagio.

"I'm not sure what it is I am looking for," I said. A friend of Kathy Weir's listened. I was at a city park in Johannesburg browsing. There were crafts, paintings, clothing, jewelry.

"These are lovely," she replied, pointing at some earrings. She walked away. Elsewhere in the park were Paul, Kathy, and another girlfriend of Kathy's.

In the distant sky were storm clouds.

Earlier in the day I joined the National Symphony musicians in order to rehearse my arrangements of traditional music. This included moving the feet with the music. Paul Bagshaw, Simon Cooper, and Joe Robinson were happy to see me. We were joined by Gabby, a bassoonist.

"This is bloody fun!" Paul responded to the feet idea.

Joe continued. "But we are going to look like bloody fools. Maybe you intend for this to be the case."

We had to move. The orchestra arrived for rehearsal. We were at the State Theater.

Paul Bagshaw was concerned.

"Look, chief. I think your arrangements are wonderful with the feet thing. Are you certain you want us? I mean we play, stomp, play, stomp. I'm not sure it will come off in any recognizable form."

I suggested we were building a bridge. After all, I would be stomping, too. I assumed there would be chaos.

"We can promise you that!" Joe chimed.

We called it a wrap. That afternoon we would go to Shoshanguve.

"I'll ride with you guys," I suggested.

A few drops of rain fell. A storm cloud was passing over the Jo'burg city park. I walked towards Paul Myburgh's Mercedes. It was on the far side of the park.

"You walk too slow, Paddy." Kathy Weir passed me. Her friend walked with her.

"He always walks slow," Kathy continued.

Kathy's friend slowed to my pace.

"I'm sorry. What is your name?" I asked.

"Norma," she replied.

I phoned Reinhold for the Shoshanguve shoot.

"I'll ride out with the musicians, Reinhold. We can run the music with the choir and have something for you to shoot."

He replied.

"We actually need to get there earlier than you to set up camera. We need to be done on time. Okay?"

There was a downpour. Deep thunder shook the Transvaal. Kathy Weir and her friend disappeared into the torrential rain to find Paul. Norma and I waited under a shelter. She leaned against the brick wall, her foot propped on the wall.

"Kathy tells me you are making a film on music in Africa."

"Actually, I am looking for a classical music and an African Mozart." She responded.

"Artists have a difficult time here. There is very little money. Will your film benefit them?"

The rain fell hard. The sky blackened.

"It might give artists deeper aspirations. I hope it might open doors for the west to hear what is now unexplored as a classical music."

She was a beautiful girl. Poised while she leaned against the wall, the rain's wind blew her shoulder length hair away from her face. She had heavy eye brows brushed by nature carefully so that her eyes were like still moonlight in a forest when late night creates heavy changing mist. Her long proportioned body spoke a hidden language a bit curious about this stranger. Bare breasts sat quietly in repose under her loose garment. There was secret longing in an African rain storm.

I wanted to tell her she was beautiful. The storm, its down pour, and the occasional earth tremors stopped me.

Schalk Visser, the musicians, and the choir had been waiting for the film crew at the Teachers College in Shoshanguve. They were not there when we arrived.

There was a phone call. It was Reinhold.

"One of our people got lost. They ended up in the wrong township."

I was not happy.

"Are you coming?"

"No. It's too late. We have a meeting."

I continued.

"What about tomorrow? Otherwise, the choir is out of school for the summer. We won't get the exchange on film."

"It's impossible. I'm sorry."

Schalk was livid.

"This is a travesty! We have all arrived when scheduled. This is an expensive loss. I can't afford to do it again."

I assured Schalk I understood.

We were to visit a children's handicapped home. Schalk's assistant asked whether I could at least visit and speak with them. "They will be disappointed," she told me.

Kathy and her friend appeared, running soaked from the rain, laughing, jumping, and turning circles in the continuing down pour.

"We can't find Paul. He must be waiting it out under a shelter."

Suddenly, there he was. As I had seen Bushmen in his film running with the same low gate chasing game, he moved the earth out of the way.

Joining the rest of us, we ran to his Mercedes.

The Philadelphia School was the school for handicapped African children. The head, a soft-spoken Afrikaner, a large gentle man, explained to me that their own tribes discarded the children.

"Tribal conflicts are replaced with the shared handicaps. The tribal dance and music is their way of sharing with each other. You will find these children understanding of your dilemma. They handle disappointment well."

"I promise I will return," I said speaking with the children.

They had gathered waiting for me.

We sat in Paul's car. He commented.

"This is a good rain. Some rains are good, some are bad. Acid rains are bad. You can feel it in the skin. This one is good. It is good to walk in."

"Weren't you concerned about the thunder, Paul?" I asked. "You were a moving target."

"Never, American! I yell back at the thunder when it yells at me. I assure you it has never, nor will it ever bother me!"

"I am sorry for today," I said to the children.

Their heads nodded with no evidence of disappointment.

"I will return. Do you accept my promise?"

They nodded. What else could they do?

AAAAAAAAAGGGGHH!!!!

Do you hear me thunder?

AAAAAAAAGGGGGHH!!!!!

CHAPTER 21
The Wind

The drive to Cape Town traveled on M1. From the Transvaal, the highway went through the Orange Free State into the Great Karoo. Finally the road passed through vineyards of the Cape Province, winding through mountains past Paarl where it tumbled into Cape Town and the sea.

The crew were Reinhold, Marlize, and Rian.

Fascinated with the southeaster and the Karoo, I had spoken of the wind as a theme to follow. My fellow travelers listened politely. Reinhold gave feedback within our 'business as usual' framework. Marlize commented when I exposed my ignorance. Rian never spoke.

Rian was a graduate of Teknikon film school. He was in his early twenties, and by outward appearance, out of his element in Pretoria. He belonged far away in Kathy Weir's Africa. I was told he was a fine poet. Blonde, handsome and physically fit. He was stoic yet hid a keen sensitivity.

He disliked me. In truth, it was not just me but who I was and where I came from. English for all Afrikaners was a second language. I learned to never underestimate the barriers created by language. For Rian, I was simply put, a foreigner. He was paid to work on African Adagio, which meant, at the very least, being hospitable to me. He was a poet from the original bush country of South Africa. As such, his gaze was always elsewhere away from cities. While the thousand year old expanse of the Great Karoo consigned my film to dust, it opened its doors to Rian. He was a son of Africa. Like Paul Myburgh and Kathy Weir, he walked with its soil under his feet, stubbornly rooted against the sky and Africa's great task maker-the sun. Rian wrote about it in Afrikanse. He could have cared less that it was understood anywhere else in the world. Soon, I would be gone. Rian would go on, miles and miles from cities, and he would not look back.

I was unprepared for the Karoo and its effect on me.

Reinhold had commented on the Karoo.

"In the winter, the stars look as though you could pluck them from the sky."

He decided we would spend the night in Beaufort West.

Small towns cropped up once in awhile traveling through the Karoo. The Karoo seemed unconcerned with their presence. The Karoo was fully capable of turning all life to dust, including a film called African Adagio.

As the sun set over the Karoo, my own insignificant history was interrupted. In a trance I was in, some impersonal definition predated the classification, homo sapien. Horizon to horizon the colors of the Karoo blended hue with hue, a never ending eye-catching dance. The hills were a prism of slow moving light. Its effect was a shock to my carefully adapted system. Strange utterances of confusing thought drifted like phantoms from an age long gone. The Karoo was a life form in itself, scrambling my species' brain like lost radio signals. The language was blessed with a simple vocabulary, an ancient one sure of its origin. My brief stint on earth meant nothing. The Karoo, a natural wonder, an unyielding beauty was the grim reaper whose unseen finger pointed to my search for the African Mozart, calling it its true name: dust to dust. At the same time it offered deep peace. The grinding sound of the van's motor buzzed civilization into my head. You must finish this....you are a civilized man from a civilized world.

As darkness fell, the Karoo silently walked into shadows of the night. Things are what they are...

"Here. Have a beer."

Reinhold placed a glass and bottle down on the table. We arrived at the Wagon Wheel motel in Beaufort West. Outside there was only quiet. In the bar a television was tuned to an evangelist. Two couples sat drinking their beers and listening to the TV.

Reinhold continued.

"We should be in Cape Town tomorrow. I need to confirm arrangements for the Cape Point shoot, but it should not be a problem."

"What do you think, Reinhold. Do we have a film yet?"

"For sure. We'll finish shooting and assemble footage to see what we have. I have stock footage for the bushmen sequence. Some cave drawings. It will be nice. I'm going in. Sleep well."

I went outside. It was midnight. Quiet now. No TV. I heard the loud crunch of stones under my shoes as I walked. I sat on a railing fence. A spring uncoiled and I dreamt. I remained here in the Karoo in the dream. It was the largest playground in the world. I heard the voices of children playing, free willed and unconcerned with tomorrow. There were those who believed Eden was in Africa, the earliest bones of man discovered in the Karoo. I was home. I lived an entire lifetime in those thirty or forty minutes.

"I can't stand up! My legs are frozen!"

A thousand wind blown feet below, gigantic waves crashed on the shoreline of Cape Point. From my dizzying view they appeared two feet high crests. In fact, they were capable of turning over a fishing vessel.

Reinhold was annoyed.

"Look. We'll tie a rope around your waist. I need this shot. Damn, man, your face is as pale as a ghost's!"

"Stop the van! I'll speak to that musician with the saxophone," I said.

Marlize had seen him. She went and returned with Daniel Khoba of Kimberley. He was cordial, slight in build, and eager to share.

"I come here to work in the streets. I will show you, if you wish," he told me.

He spent the day with me. Crowds gathered when he played. The music bounced with a light contagious melody. His sax was old and needed repair, but his music was honest.

He was candid.

"A musician's life is difficult. I am away from home for many days. What I am doing is important for my children. You see, music is Africa. Perhaps you have noticed this. People come up to me. They say, 'play your horn!' They grab my arm! Musicians will bring all peoples of South Africa together one day into one big ball. I was born Sotho, but my music is Africa. When I return home to Kimberley I bring presents to my children. They see that their father is happy. God has blessed us, brother, with our music. We cannot hold this inside. The joy must come out. Musicians will change the heart of Africa. You will see."

"You and that little kaffir have become good friends, eh?"

The comment from the crew stung me. I was hourly losing grip on reality. I was not certain whether it was in fact wished or planned for me to fall off the cliff at Cape Point. I was left on my own when we weren't shooting.

"It was a perfect shot! Yes, I was very angry," Reinhold said.

"I apologize, Reinhold. I was not clear why you wanted it. I assumed there would be other people in the shot."

He was livid.

"Then I would have had tourists! Damn. I'll get over it. The camera is my art, and you got in its way. If you had fallen off the cliff and I got my shot, I would have been contented getting the shot. You Americans have to have doubles. You have to have someone else take the risks. It's nothing for us to take risks. We take hundreds of risks. The fact that you were surprised I asked you to take a risk makes you a foreigner. Fuck, man, you can't even stand on a simple cliff."

I spent the evening with Reinhold's sister while he was elsewhere. She was a woman my age. Shy, soft spoken, her conversation reflected quality, yet at the same time loneliness. She had suffered. She shared with me why.

"I was a social worker in District Six, the Malay Quarter, prior to the Verwoerd government's resettlement of the Malay. There was high crime at the time. Still, it was evil what the government did. You know, I have visited the United States. I like Americans. They have a true compassion at times. When it came to understanding other societies, though, I often found ignorance."

I asked whether this disturbed her.

"No. It doesn't. You would have to live in South Africa for a very long time in order to understand. These people are not bad, really. They are trying to be a western society when they are not one. Those who truly love this country tell the truth. They are usually ostracized, or imprisoned."

Later, Reinhold picked me up. Driving away I told him I was deeply impressed with his sister.

He was quiet at first. Then he spoke.

"My sister went to jail for her outspoken views against the government relocating the Malay in District Six. The government told her to be quiet, but she wouldn't. She was arrested, went to trial, and was convicted. Except for me, our family did not support her."

He said nothing else. I understood his anger at me for not taking risks.

"Tourism ripped my people off!"

Cedric John Adamson was railing at Reinhold as we filmed the Malay singers.

"None of my people were paid. No one saw a dime from tourism." Reinhold snapped back.

"I did that film! We asked your representative what it would cost, and the money was sent. It is in my records. Come and see for yourself!"

Later after we left Reinhold had more to say.

"I didn't rip them off. Some fucking coon took the money and disappeared. If you want to work with someone like Cedric Adamson who won't even check out whether there are crooks in his outfit, do so without me!"

When we left Cape Town we raced against time in order to get to the Karoo for the closing shot. An hour before sunset, Reinhold told Rian to pull off onto an unpaved road in the Karoo.

"Okay. You have one take to say what you have to say."

He set up the camera and sound.

"Rolling....sound....go..."

"In the early 1800's at the turn of the Century, Napoleon Bonaparte entered Moscow for one of the decisive meetings in history. There are those who believe that the outcome was determined by the generals not the common soldier. Leo Tolstoy in War and Peace wrote that it was the common soldier who defeated Napoleon. The people in this film are not generals. They are ordinary individuals. They are not famous, but they dream to be. From this dreaming, the common individual, Tolstoy's hero, dreams of being a Beethoven, a Mozart, an Ellington. Here in the Great Karoo, such a dream is born or disappears into thin air. Perhaps the southeaster will carry this dream across South Africa, Mozambique, Zimbabwe, Namibia, over all of southern Africa. After all, in the words of an Afrikaner song writer...these are the children of the wind."

"Cut!"

Reinhold swung the camera facing the setting sun. There was a scurry of equipment and lens settings. I watched Reinhold film the setting sun over the Karoo. He was filming what he knew best. Braced against his camera, eye to the lens, he worked slowly in sync with a land he knew better than most men. I had made my comments and I was out of his way. Reinhold, Marlize, and Rian were free of me. They were with their setting sun, one that would remain with them long after I had gone.

After Cape Town I felt I had made a mistake. These people did not need me or America.

CHAPTER 22
Return to Shoshanguve

Arrangements were made from Schalk's office once more for the exchange between the musicians from the National Symphony and the Technical Teachers College choir in Shoshanguve. The quartet, Paul, Simon, Joe, and Gabby were joined with African drummer, Lulu Tsheola and singer, Isabella Mosote.

This time I rode with the film crew. Outside the State Theater I waited for their van. Rian drove up with Marlize. They were unusually quiet. I asked whether there was a problem. Marlize responded.

"Reinhold will tell you."

I protested. Had the film been canceled? Again, Marlize insisted that I must speak to Reinhold.

Philip Hattingh and Reinhold finally arrived. Reinhold's news was devastating.

"Tourism has disbanded the film unit. I was told this morning they are closing us down." Philip continued in a stoic manner belying their collective disgust.

"How are things going? I'll be ready to assemble your film next week. See you then."

It was a bizarre moment. *African Adagio* would be the last film made with tourism. Was this the cause of the shut down?

The drive to Shoshanguve was anything but festive. It was an uncomfortably quiet drive.

We entered the township watching children going home from school. They were dressed in the same blue uniform and white blouse. Small houses lined the streets where there was not a blade of grass. Women walked slowly along the roadside, balancing large bundles on their heads. The Teachers Training College was surrounded by tall dry grass. It was a beautiful late summer day.

At the Teachers Training College the musicians and I rehearsed the arrangements. When the choir entered the room they were visibly taken aback. Classical musicians were playing tribal wedding songs, swaying and stomping their feet.

I introduced our group and suggested we combine the choir with the instruments. The singers in the choir looked at me, and seemed to want the nearest exit. We began as I suggested. I conducted with heartfelt zeal. How could this choir not know they were making history? Their conductor came up to me after the first attempt. He was intimidated speaking to me, but he was polite.

"Perhaps, first, you could listen as we sing this song. Indeed, it would be better if you could bring it down a key?"

Chaos ensued. This piece of tribal wedding music turned two cultures upside down, made worse by the fact that I kept saying, "loosen up, it's an exchange, a new idea." I was excited. I had come 8000 miles in order to experience this moment. I was lost, but never happier. We imitated Africa, looked their way, and we took the time to look their way.

When the choir sang alone I noticed the conductor swaying, moving the music into his body. The choir swayed and stomped with equal grace, unconcerned with the limitations our instruments had. Here was the bridge!

For the first time it all made sense to me. Paul Myburgh had counseled; *Music must go from your head, where you are in a habit of, to your body, where you are dead.* He insisted I must stop thinking of solutions that others steal before they have a chance to live. "Life is long," he said, "Live."

Of course! I would start the song with the musicians, turn it over to the choir's conductor, and get out of the way. He would lead all of us to the music! He was extremely uncomfortable. He had never led a group of white musicians, particularly leading them with African song.

Thus, an African choirmaster conducted members of the National Symphony with the first attempt to bring into being a classical music from Africa. The room filled with the light of dawn. Western trained classical musicians took their first steps toward the continent of Africa. We had always walked on her soil, and taken from it. On this day in Shoshanguve we were broken by the music and we felt Africa. We were givers.

"This was great, chief," Paul Bagshaw remarked afterwards.

"One of the choir members told us they felt they sang better with us playing. Imagine that! So, how do you think we did, chief?"

I told him that they had proven a hunch. I was indebted to them.

The film crew were silent. They were not on the same page, too shaken from losing their jobs. They filmed it. That was all. When I pointed out the unique fruits of the exchange, the history making aspect, they remained quiet and unresponsive. It was clear they wondered whether my happiness was worth the price they had paid.

Lulu Tsheola, the drummer, rode with me back to Pretoria.

I asked him what the name of the song was that we had played and sung. Was there a title?

"It is a Sotho song. It is called, *Seana Marena*. It means, *it makes the kings happy*."

CHAPTER 23
Musicians from Bloemfontein

Schalk Visser was glad to see me. He was elated with my report, he, the only one who understood the history making outcome in Shoshanguve. He knew I had achieved my goal, and he knew what it meant to South African music. Without Shoshanguve, the African Mozart would remain a myth. The exchange was an important step, albeit a small one. Black classical musicians would one day open the doors. We felt that after Shoshanguve that was a day in the near future.

He suggested we celebrate. A group of classical musicians from Bloemfontein in the Orange Free State were giving a recital that evening, and he thought it would be an appropriate way to end the day.

The concert was at Pretoria University.

When the musicians began playing, neither Schalk nor I moved a muscle. Turina, Dvorak, and Brahms F minor quartet were on the program.

For two hours war ceased. Schalk and I could have been anywhere in the world. What peace in contrast to my self-possessed prison. Too heavy a physical and emotional price had been paid for an historical moment that had neither political nor commercial power. Outside of my friend, Schalk Visser, few listened and celebrated the role of music for peace.

After the concert Schalk invited me to the reception for the quartet at a restaurant.

Sitting next to me was Michael Haller, the cellist. His family had immigrated to South Africa when he was a 10. I asked him whether he, too, experienced dark moods living as a classical musician. He confessed that when the cello was his god there were very dark times.

There was something different about all of these musicians, as if music was in service to a mission that warranted deeper commitment and produced a peace that passed understanding. From these musicians I heard words that shook the core of my being.

I shared what had happened in Shoshanguve, and the implications it had for the future and black classical musicians with African classical music.

John Wille, the violist, told me that there were presently African classical musicians in the Soweto township! They had played with them in Lesotho. He admitted they went with the attitude that they would help the township players, but left, having instead, an equal exchange. Michael Haller continued.

"We had with us a young cellist who hated the idea of playing with blacks. During the rehearsal a Soweto clarinetist, a young woman, announced that her part was not transposed for her Bflat clarinet. Our cellist rudely commented that the Soweto clarinetist, "will never be able to transpose it on sight." The young clarinetist said nothing. She played, sight reading, and transposed the music perfectly! More remarkable, we had no oboe player. The Soweto trumpet player said he could play the oboe part on the trumpet. To all of our surprise, he played the oboe part, transposing it for his Bflat trumpet, and made his trumpet sound like an oboe!"

They insisted I should get in contact with the Soweto musicians. The phone number and the name of the contact person they would send me once they returned to Bloemfontein. Then, too my surprise, the musicians gathered in a circle around me. They wanted to pray for me. They prayed that God would bless the seed from Shoshanguve, and that a music from Africa would bring a new peace. There was an indefinable affect this prayer had on me in the days to come. Mixed with my increasing doubts a blind faith promised the end to my journey.

Following their moving prayer, vision came from losing sight and having to walk in darkness. My strength continued to wear thin. Personal demons bore down on my insecurity. The suffering of so many around me reduced the African Mozart to vanity, all is vanity saith the preacher. South Africa had so many brothers of men killing and maiming. Armed resistance resulting in hundreds of deaths. My presence was so utterly unimportant. Yet, something beyond my importance and suffering lived. A prayer guaranteed that the yet to be seen would survive.

A few nights later I was alone at Anna Marie Englebrecht's house. Something snapped inside. A coiled spring enduring badly the daily turmoil came off its hinges. Bodily chills came with no apparent fever. My heart pounded violently. No pleasant thoughts or breathing could calm me. Reading a book, sentences passed by without comprehension.

Two hours. Three hours. It was a nightmare I could not escape.

No one must know! Be strong! Call no one... Say nothing...

"There is strength in being alone," I remembered Paul Myburgh's words.

I sat at the piano to play some Mozart sonatas. These simple balanced melodies of musical perfection came out brittle and motionless.

Music..words...time...reality....cold, ice cold!

Stop! It is time to stop! Tonight your world dies. The river is flooding. There is no rescue. There is only the abyss. All else is illusion!

By midnight it was all madness. A jumble. *African Adagio, Cape Town, New York, the Karoo, Tolstoy, dance music, Shakespeare, Mendelssohn, Mahler, air travel, unpaid bills, the Amazon, racial violence, prayers,* and missing from all of it...love. Love and South Africa.

When early morning came, I was emotionally and spiritually spent. Beaten up, bruised, I was awaked by the African sun.

In my notes I found the name sent to me by Michael Haller from Bloemfontein. Lindumutze MnGoma. There was a phone number. I hesitated, defeated. I made some coffee, and poured a cup. I stared at the note with the phone number. I lit a cigarette. I finished my coffee and put out the cigarette. I walked to the window in the living room and looked out of the window blankly. I looked once more at the note. Finally, I picked up the phone. I dialed. A man answered. I introduced myself.

"Mr. MnGoma, I am from the United States, I am a composer. I believe I might be of some assistance to you. Can you come to where I am staying in Johannesburg and allow me to share with you my thoughts?"

He said he would come that morning.

The season was turning to South African winter. Evenings were cooler than all of the others I had known in South Africa. I was ill prepared for this season and its sharp contrasts.

CHAPTER 24
Lindumutze MnGoma

It was midday when Lindumutze MnGoma drove his motorcycle up to the gate of the Englebrecht home. I looked out of the living room window and watched an exchange between him and Angelina, their housekeeper. He parked his motorcycle on the side of the house.

We shook hands and sat in the living room. Angelina went into the kitchen to prepare tea. Lindu was English-speaking and Zulu. It was immediately clear from the beginning that he was a knowledgeable classical musician. He was a cellist.

Angelina brought the tea nearly tripping over Lindu. Giggling, she ran out of the room. I excused myself and followed her into the kitchen. I asked whether she knew Lindu.

"No. I don't," she answered.

Lindumutze MnGoma was medium height, solid framed, and had a broad, handsome face with a graying goatee. He had warm, smiling eyes.

"Who is that man?" Angelina asked.

"Is he, perhaps, married?"

I told her I thought that he was.

"That is too bad," she smiled.

Did she like him?

"I l-o-v-e that man!" she exclaimed.

I was up front with Lindu. I told him about the tourism film, the State Theater, the experience in Shoshanguve, and the contact given through the musicians from Bloemfontein. I confessed that I was surprised classical musicians existed in the townships. It meant to me that an African classical music must exist. I shared my feelings about an African Mozart. I fully expected to be told it was too European a view.

Lindu smiled from ear to ear. He laughed a large laugh.

"It has been a dream of many for a long time. My father was the head of music at a school in Zululand. For years he trained many string players. The talent and an the orchestra is here and waiting to become a part of the classical music world."

I shared the fact that Bela Bartok had spent years collecting the folk melodies of Hungary. His work rested securely in classical music, as did the folk melodies. There was precedent for a similar music for Africa. He responded enthusiastically.

"This explains something. When we teach the young people classical music through singing, they have trouble with much of classical music, with the exception of Bartok. They easily learn and remember his melodies. They respond well to folk melodies."

I asked Lindu about the orchestra.

" Presently, we have a group of 16 musicians that regularly meet in Soweto. We are in need of better instruments, a rehearsal space, and transport to concerts."

I nervously inquired whether it would be possible for me to come to a rehearsal. Both of us understood the problems with this request. Soweto was off limits to whites.

"I will look into it. I believe it is possible. Understand that we are not yet a fully fledged symphony orchestra. Discipline often is a problem. Our players need improvement with their execution of the music."

I assured Lindu their mere existence far outweighed my concerns about orchestral excellence. It was an inspiring day just sitting with him and hearing they existed at all. He, too, was equally enthusiastic.

"This offer of yours is momentous for us. My father dedicated his life to what you came so far to find. We have always been here. That it took someone from so far away to come and discover us is overwhelming."

I confessed that it had been a long and trying journey. It was worth it now. I hoped I could be of genuine assistance, at the very least a friend for the creation of African classical music.

"Such a day is already here," he said. "Many children visit each other's schools and share their dream of this music."

I could feel blood returning to my face.

Paul Myburgh and Kathy Weir were stunned by my news.
"A classical orchestra in Soweto!" he said.
They were eager to hear the details. Smiling and teasing he responded.
"I suppose you will need someone to take you to Soweto."
We were excited, and I credited the excitement with his Africa.
"His Africa!" Kathy yelled, " I was the first to show you, Paddy!"

Lindumutze phoned me and extended the invitation to come to a rehearsal. It was night when Paul Myburgh, Kathy Weir, and I drove into Soweto in Paul's Mercedes whose doors were yet to be closed without slamming them.

To get to Soweto we drove on Empire Road, then took M1 south. Twenty minutes passed by. On the right side of the highway was the sprawling massive community of Soweto. Once inside, in a very short time we were lost. Kathy was concerned. Soweto was a dangerous place with gangs of youth roaming the dark streets. Paul had been chased by a gang once only to run into the police coming from the other direction. The road we were on was asphalt paved. Small boxed houses were on both sides of the street. There was the smell of burning coal fires. Resisting apartheid, residents did not pay electric bills, and with electricity cut off, there was no light. Coal was burnt for warmth, light, and cooking.

A truck passed us and stopped at a red light. Paul's Mercedes pulled up in back of the truck. He went to speak to the driver. The resulting quiet was unsettling. There was now no safety of South African police. We were illegally in Soweto.

Paul was gone for a long time. Kathy was frightened. It was her first trip to Soweto. We were in the heart of her Africa and trembling.

Paul returned and started the Mercedes engine, following the truck. The truck lead us to the Funda Art Center.

The darkness increased. Soon the roads were unpaved. Through large open fields with no trees, no grass, no buildings, we passed into the void. More crowded housing followed. There were no phones, no gas stations. We were in the heart of Soweto. Violence in the townships had increased in news reports that month.

On the outskirts of Soweto, the Funda Art Center came into view. The truck driver signaled and went on. Paul drove through the gates. In the center were recently built one story brick buildings.

I stepped out of the Mercedes. In the night sky I could see the Southern Cross through the smoke of coal fires. I heard Bach coming from one of the buildings. All three of us were still, not moving. Surrounded by the history of Soweto we heard the 300 year old counterpoint of history's greatest master of music, a prophet for peace and order.

Paul Myburgh, who had lived in the Kalahari, was awed. Kathy Weir and her African innocence had always loved the secrets of Africa's culture. This was too much to absorb. It was incongruent. I, her Martian, had first introduced her to Chopin on a broken pair of earphones at a record shop in Pretoria. But Soweto?

I was beside myself. The bumbling, incoherent fool. I could not believe what I was hearing!

We walked to the building and entered, following the music of Bach. In a small rehearsal room we found 12 musicians. Violins, violas, celli, flutes, a clarinet, a trumpet, a group of Africans dispelling the limited and grossly unfair view of a people "only good at star gazing".

Faces read concern. Who were we?

As the rehearsal ended, Lindumutze MnGoma stood and introduced me. My pulse raced, my palms sweat. I spoke.

"Ladies and gentlemen. I have been looking for you for a long time. Before now, I believed you to be a vision of the future. I am from the United States and I would like to be of some assistance. Would you be interested?"

Sandele Khemese, the orchestra's concert master and leader spoke.

"Could you join us this Sunday?"

I was honored and accepted his invitation. I asked whether they played any chamber music. Sandele offered a suggestion.

"Do you know Mendelssohn's Trio in D minor?"

I had known it for years. We would play it Sunday.

I was approached by Samkelo Khumalo. He was a reporter for Drum Publications. He asked for the phone number where I was staying. He wanted to call later and interview me.

Paul Myburgh later told me Drum Publications was the newspaper that had been the voice for South African struggle. Black leaders, resisting apartheid, had been affiliated with the paper. He shared with me a film called *Drum*. It was a documentary relating these people's tenacity and courage.

We would return to Soweto April 30, 1989 at 10 a.m.

CHAPTER 25
The Bliss of Africa

It was a sun-washed morning, April 30, 1989. Paul Myburgh and I drove to Soweto. Paul planned to observe the rehearsal. He would look for a structure for the film. We once again were lost. Paul pulled into the gate of an army post. A soldier stood at the gate with his gear. Paul asked directions. The soldier did not know, but asked to be driven through the camp to the other gate.

They were typical army barracks, functional for training and military maneuvers. Open fields, bunk houses, very little foliage. It was army.

"Bae danke!" the soldier thanked us in Afrikanse. Paul returned to the gate we had entered. The barracks seemed deserted.

"Can you believe we are driving through without clearance?" Paul commented.

"If we were up to no good, it would be a cinch!"

Eventually we found the Funda Art Center. There was a buzz of activity that morning. Choirs prepared for rehearsals. Our presence caused at first curiosity, then apathy.

When we found the musicians, they were rehearsing. Sandi and his brother, Malusi, were playing through the Mendelssohn D minor Trio. The console piano was rolled in from the larger rehearsal room to a smaller studio. Sandi played from memory. The cello part had not been found, so Malusi was playing from a xeroxed copy of the score.

We played. Sandi's tone was clear and expressive. His technique was excellent. Malusi was a bit more timid, but his musicianship easily found what was needed. My piano playing had seen better days. I had not played piano the weeks filming African Adagio. The thrill of that moment carried the day. The small practice room filled with the romanticism of Mendelssohn, a flame in sound burning in Soweto where fires of a different nature had burned since 1976. We continued with the reverent second movement. Sandi and Malusi were behind me, the piano facing the wall. There were tears in my eyes. Mendelssohn, champion of J.S. Bach. His trio was being played in Soweto, championing new heroes. A greeting, a welcoming, a beacon of hope. This great-great grandfather, a resurrection on a continent whose own song was yet to sprout from the soil in Africa. Paul quietly leaned on the wall and listened.

In time, the remainder of the orchestra arrived in the rehearsal space. The piano was moved back to the orchestra room. Lindu greeted me.

You are in the paper this morning.

He gave me the copy of City Press. Such Talent Must Not Die, the headline read. The search for an African Mozart now played a small part in the history of Soweto.

The rehearsal began. I created a piano part from the conductor's score. Then we continued with Bach. I took a violin part and a cello part and created a continuo. Sandi conducted with his bow establishing tempi. He would stop the orchestra to make corrections. The more we played, intonation sharpened. Notes found their correct execution.

They needed time they did not have. The fact was: they existed. They wanted to develop a vehicle for classical works from their ranks. Could they bridge the differences and reach out from Soweto to the rest of the classical world?

We took a break and went for coffee and beers. Cyril Khumalo, the trumpet player, expressed his concerns.

"The problem is that there is no consistent musical notation. Without that a regular understanding of African music performance is impossible."

I wondered whether using Zulu, Xhosa or other Abantu expressions would clarify notation. Certainly the French, German, Italian composers had a long tradition of doing this very thing.

We discussed the African triplet, different in execution from all other musical triplets. "What if it could be adapted to a simple symbol, that once recordings were available, conductors and other classical musicians could identify its unique musical quality?"

These were promising ideas to Cyril.

"My brother has had quite a bit of success writing our music for performance. Unfortunately, one of his pieces was interpreted as politically subversive and he was taken to jail by the apartheid apparatus."

Sandi related a story that remains for me an heroic tale.

"We played in Scotland at the International String Quartet Festival. They announced the quartets who were participating and where they were from. Our name, the Soweto String Quartet, was immediately given a standing ovation. When we played, our playing was not up to the standard of many of the quartets there, but again we were given a standing ovation. We had learned our Beethoven by candle light. A string quartet from Bloemfontein was also at the festival. One of their players came up to me and snapped, 'wait until we get back to South Africa, kaffir. A jail is waiting for you!' Fortunately, I was offered a bursary to study in England where I could have opted for British citizenship. I decided to return to Soweto. There were children waiting to be taught. I came home and have remained here."

Paul listened to these stories and conceived of making a film that included the musicians from the National Symphony. Paul knew that these musicians were eager to share. I asked Sandi, Lindu, and Cyril whether this would be a problem for them. It wasn't.

"We have played often played with National Symphony musicians and others who are supportive of us. Perhaps this will be the bridge you speak of."

All of my suggestions had been dreams and visions of theirs for a long time. Lack of funds and public interest, or knowledge of their existence, had kept doors shut. I was assured my interest was a crucial development.

"You support a venture that is more than a dream. We exist. We are real and we have a viable struggle," Sandi remarked.

"We have always been here," Cyril Khumalo continued, "no one, simply put, has cared."

Among these fellow classical musicians I was welcomed as if I were a ship arriving in a harbor whose people had seen too many ships pass by on their way to more established ports.

"I know what I want to do with this," Paul Myburgh said as we were on our way back to Jo'burg.

"I'll shoot some cut away scenes of life in Soweto. While you, Sandi, and Malusi play in the small room I will pan the camera from outside the building looking into the window of the room as if to say, 'what is this?' You must arrange for the musicians from Pretoria to be there. We can shoot this next Sunday."

I agreed to call them.

Meanwhile, I had not been ready to end music making. I invited everyone to Anna Marie Englebrecht's house to play. When I arrived, Johann was preparing to leave for another South African Airways flight to New York. It had slipped my mind that I was only a guest in their home when I invited 12 musicians. Johann was generous, accepting the use of their home for music making.

Many of the players soon arrived, some with wives and children. I took requests for beer or tea. It was conditional that no one call me 'baas'. Returning with beverages, the room broke out in chorus.

"Thank you, baas!"

We played. That afternoon we became a musical family making music for over two and one half hours. I began the 12 bar blues, and was joined, everyone laughing with joy that bounced off of the walls. Then I began Seana Marena. It was, of course, known.

At some point, Kathy Weir and Paul Myburgh had entered the room. Paul positioned himself next to the piano where he studied us intently while we drifted from one musical conversation to the next.

Soon the day of days ended. It was a parting of sweet sorrow. We would be together again the following Sunday.

Later that evening at Paul's home in Melville I played a cassette recording I had made of the afternoon.

"This is stunning," Kathy Weir commented.

"The African tune you played did not sound African," Paul remarked.

I was crestfallen. I was under the impression it had. I had been immersed in the music I had waited so long to play with classical musicians.

Later I asked Lindu on the phone about Paul's criticism.

He laughed.

"We were following you, Patrick!"

They were being polite.

"This is wonderful news," Schalk Visser exclaimed when I called him.

"I wish that they would audition for the National Orchestra. It is particularly wonderful that you are inviting Paul Bagshaw and the others. I only wish I could be there. I am sure it will be a wonderful exchange. Keep me posted."

Schalk knew it was against the law for gatherings not approved in Soweto. I was never sure of anything I did, legal or not, in South Africa. I was certain of Schalk Visser's trust in me, and to this day assume he quietly made arrangements for me to be legally in Soweto without any fanfare.

Of all the people in this story, only Schalk understood what this meant historically to classical music. With him, bridges could be built out of harms way. Without him, African classical music had no true father figure.

I called Paul Bagshaw. He left me a note:

Dear Paddy baby, we're hip to the gig, man, on the sabbath moon for the goat sacrifice. We await your transport details,etc., with eager anticipation, yet trepidation. We're cool if you're cool. Peace, bro!

I forgot to contact them later. When I did it was too late. I called Paul Myburgh. He was not happy.

"But this film hangs on them! Can you get them for the following Sunday. I'll shoot the Soweto musicians with you this Sunday."

I called Paul Bagshaw. That would work. They could do it.

CHAPTER 26
Filming in Soweto

Sunday, May 7, 6:30 a.m. I had been awake for thirty minutes. I spent the night at Paul Myburgh's. I heard Paul's alarm buzz. Working at Tangori Chicken until 2 a.m., he was normally a late sleeper.

"Coffee?" Paul asked.

"Forget your star status. You're a gofer this morning," he said.

Paul wanted the early morning sun in Soweto, so we loaded the Mercedes. Paul, Kathy, and Andy, Paul's assistant, prepared for the drive to Soweto. Andy was mild mannered, a prerequisite working with Paul Myburgh. A misplaced cable meant a bad shot, albeit human error. It was not tolerated with Paul. He spent time on subject matter, not error. Paul did not like chaos.

We were strange bedfellows. As was the case in Shoshanguve, my process involved tossing a firecracker into the hen house, stirring up chaos. I thrived on it. The simple act of carrying a mike boom to the Mercedes was a difficult task for me.

It was ideal weather for a shoot. We drove into Soweto. The citizens were out and about in large gatherings. People congregated on street corners, others chatted over the fences of yards. Soweto was alive at 8 a.m.

We drove passed an empty lot to a traffic island. The corner was littered with old tires, and consumer refuse, home to a few trees, some bushes, and patches of brown grass. Laughter came easily from ordered, shanty houses. Passerbys exchanged morning greetings to neighbors working in gardens.

Paul stopped, and with Andy and Kathy, went to work. I went to buy a City Press. A brick one story warehouse extended half a block. It was a grocery, a single large room with a low ceiling and several long isles of groceries. The customer line in the store was long, but it moved swiftly.

I left the store and went outside. I heard people yelling at the film crew.

"Point the camera here! Here! This way!"

A car drove by with hands waving out of the window.

Paul looked away from his lens. His concentration had been broken. He pointed.

"Look. Those boys over there. The home made toys."

Two six or seven year old boys played with arrows and bows made with tree branches, electrician tape, and wire. Another pushed the rim of a bike with a stick, rolling It over bumpy pavement.

Paul moved farther down the street to an empty lot. His camera respected its subject. He searched for shots without the need to trash a subject with dramatic reenactment. He was both instinctual and intellectual. If humor came, it came out of the day: two boys aiming home made arrows at birds and misfiring, or shouting adults concerned over the misfired twig.

We moved on. Paul turned off the road to an unpaved street. Here was the classical view of Soweto. Concrete box houses with one or two rooms, and occasionally two box houses within a fence with simple latched gates. There were no curbs. Children played outdoors within the fenced yard. A woman swept the debris in the street with a broom made from a bundle of straw.

"We are going around the corner to film some traffic. Stay with the car," Paul instructed .

I lit my pipe. Disgusted with my pipe tobacco, Paul had given me an aromatic blend he had made. The aroma mixed with the morning air, clearing from a night of coal fires.

Four small children under five stared at me from a yard. I said good morning. I had pocket change, and offered it. They smiled. A man came from the house, saw me speaking with the children and walked up to me.

"Are you from the SABC?"

"No, I am from the United States," I answered.

"America! I do Elvis," he told me.

He went back inside his house and returned with a photo album.

"Many say that when I do Elvis, I look like him. I teach the children to do Elvis in my neighborhood. These articles call me the Soweto Elvis. May I dance for you?"

He went back inside and placed speakers in the window. Out of the window came the voice of Elvis Presley.

A reverie from long ago drifted into consciousness.

On a soft summer night in Higgston, Georgia, Ishmael Jackson West had fixed a party game. I won a walk with Linda, the prettiest girl at the party, a girl Jack knew I liked. Walking along the highway to Vidalia, her hands brushed mine. Her flowered dress blew over my pants leg. She walked to my rhythm. The walk lasted forever, forever beginning that night.

Later I wrote to her. She wrote me only one letter. She told me that she planned to marry Elvis Presley. I was second fiddle, a distant one. Of course, she never married Elvis. Years passed before I figured out that Ishmael Jackson West had set the whole thing up.

When Elvis boomed out of the window in Soweto, everyone was doing Elvis. A fourteen year old dreamer at a party in Georgia, a Soweto Elvis, and children of the Soweto Elvis swaying their hips to the music.

When the music ended I turned to see Paul and his camera. Like some ancient sage, Paul Myburgh seemed to find the soul of a camera. He had filmed the Soweto Elvis and the Higgston, Georgia wannabe. It was Africa with all of its unpredictable turns in the road, that Kathy Weir had wanted me to see that first night in Hillbrow, when I had asked for a single story. She had been silent then, looking off into her Africa far away from that airport bar.

I had asked Paul Myburgh the night I met him at Rocky Street in Hillbrow whether he would take me to see the Bushmen. "I don't know you well enough," he had responded.

Now both of them were smiling, watching me with the Soweto Elvis.

Paul and I were enchanted with this untamable girl. Both of us deeply loved her.

I had told Kathy Weir one evening, that for the remainder of my life, she would have a place deep in my heart. I would always love her.

"I feel the same," she cautiously responded. It was the same caution she had had returning the frisbee at the film school the first time I saw her.

I told her I wanted to share a deeper feeling. I begged her to try and hear me. I said that she had chosen eagles, and she had a special gift to give them courage to fly in uncharted places. I felt that she must not look back once they had flown on. If she did, the effervescent beauty that made her unique would fade into deep sadness.

Loving Kathy Weir was like loving the Great Kalahari. It was unto itself a life form.

The three of us were friends with unusual pasts. The future promised much the same.

At the Funda Art Center it was one o'clock before we had the rehearsal space. It was fortuitous that the National Symphony musicians had been rescheduled. They would have had to leave at noon.

All afternoon the camera rolled. The film crew and the musicians filled the hours from 1p.m., until we called it a day at 5 p.m. No tempers flared. Patience was eternal. The music was Bach. Next gathering, it would be the Soweto musicians, the musicians from the National Symphony and Seana Marena.

When man walked out of the garden of Eden, it was a long walk to the Euphrates and the cradle of civilization. Years passed and memory faded into the form of a fable until man drowned in knowledge.

There is a song in the soil of Africa. It is an important one. There is no way in God's green continent we could march in our little ordered ranks to this music. With this song, the west would only be able to dance, our bare feet pounding the earth, shaking the multitudes of skyscrapers, cracking the pavements of the streets, toppling the factories and their billowing smoke stacks, awakening the natural mineral life in the soil, plants, flowers, forests, their roots vibrating to the rich rhythmic pulse of a song and its dance, purifying the air until the sun is in harmony once again with the thin layer of atmosphere caring for sea, land, and the earth's multitudes. Not the power of man singing and dancing, but the power of the music and its expression in our bodies and the earth.

But no. *That's it, West....one...two...three....four....forward march! Get those feet in line.....those thoughts in order.......those theologies scripturally founded..........those theories in line with political thought.......March! Your youth beat their brains with a music made with metal and electricity....beating the air with their bodies....crying, Damn you! We don't want to march anymore! Beat the air, young! Scream...soon the earth will speak.*

Earthquakes. Sing, fools! Tornadoes, hurricanes. Dance! Pound the earth! Give the soil our body's rhythm not its refuse.

It won't happen. We will not listen to the song.

The Messiah is supposed to return on horseback. Horseback? Some fable, for sure. We have air travel. Horses pound the earth, though. A song in the soil of Africa would awaken us from the Euphrates all the way to the land of gold, from Zimbabwe to Cape Town. Then the West could hear!

There would be a thousand years of peace. That is my fable.

1986 a girl named Kathy took my hand to see her Africa. 1989 in Soweto the laughter of children mixed with the sounds of classical musicians from Soweto. I had found those, like Mozart had done for the West, who could bring out from bondage the songs written in the native tongue, rescued from both apartheid and western arrogance. Here was true music, true deliverance, and true unconditional love.

Soon I could go home.

CHAPTER 27
The Last Hours

I had spent the night at Reinhold Thaumuller's in Pretoria. African Adagio had its first cut, and Reinhold and I discussed plans for its airing, once I returned to the United States.

Two of the National Symphony Musicians picked me up for the drive to Soweto, about one hour from Pretoria. It was one of the most beautiful sunny mornings I had awakened to in South Africa.

At the entrance to Soweto we met Paul Bagshaw and Simon Cooper.

"You know, Paul came down with the bloody dysentery last night," Simon said leaning into the car window. Paul Bagshaw came up to the car. I asked if he was okay.

"I'm better. I spent the night blowing it out of both ends, but I didn't want to disappoint you, chief!"

None of these musicians had ever been to Soweto. Prior to that morning we had already been on a long road together: Mamelodi, where they first had the idea I should make some arrangements, then the mishap in Shoshanguve, and finally, the historical moment in Shoshanguve where classical music reached towards Africa. Now we were in Soweto where they would meet fellow classical musicians, and one more time play the foot stomping arrangement of Seana Marena, 'it makes the kings happy'.

At the Funda Art Center I made the introductions. Paul, Kathy, and Andy had not yet arrived. The orchestra was first and second violins, viola, celli, flute, clarinet, oboe, bassoon, and trumpet. It was a classical orchestra of Wolfgang Amadeus Mozart's day.

Paul and film crew finally arrived. Soon we were ready. Camera and musicians from Soweto, musicians from Pretoria, and a musician from the United States took our steps toward African classical music. It proved a day of unforgettable musical exploration, emerging from the unique freedom classical music owns, through its knowledge and its language.

Lindumutze MnGoma stood. He illustrated body movement from the feet notations I had scribbled in the score. Quavers changed to semi quavers, executing far more flexible, less rigid music. The discussion of the African triplet continued, this time among classical musicians who understood it and classical musicians who wanted to understand it.

Seana Marena was played as I had first written the music. All of us stood. We moved with Lindu. More changes. We played again. Again and again. We listened to Lindu, Sandi, and the other members of the Soweto orchestra. There was self-effacing humor. The reach towards Africa was not without comedy. The small rehearsal hall on the outskirts of Soweto, South Africa, filled with a music and a human energy that climbed plateau after plateau through careful, hard work.

Paul, Kathy, and Andy climbed through the musicians tied to each other with cables. Like mobile scribes they filmed each struggle.

Musicians and a film crew untangled lines and chords reaching the apex of this day in Soweto. The musicians from Pretoria ripped to shreds the last vestiges of apartheid from the music and hearts of their fellow classical musicians in Soweto. A musician from the United States re-scored western notation until his notes on a page got out of the way of a song from Africa.

Those present saw the promised land. The musicians from Muse Africa Muse Symphony could walk in it and claim it for new generations of African musicians.

We were humbled. We felt deeply that this would be the source for new works of classical music from Africa composed by South African composers, and introduced to the world through a united effort. This new music, its movement through the body, and its vitality, would win the praise of audiences, lasting beyond the words of short sighted critics.

No one was the same when the day ended. There was a shared sense of common purpose. Something of great magnitude had occurred. All of us experienced a resurrection, rebirth: a music with promise for peace and a new South Africa, a gift to the world tangled in knots of war and bloodshed.

The musicians from Pretoria prepared to leave and return to their homes. I told them how fortune had smiled on me the day I met them. I thanked them for following me through the journey. Paul Bagshaw spoke.

"Look, chief, it was our pleasure. You've done something special for us. If you ever need us again, we are here. We will definitely miss seeing you in South Africa!"

Paul Myburgh invited the Soweto musicians to Tangori Chicken for a post filming celebration in Hillbrow. Paul, the astute businessman, was getting nothing from this thus far, paying for the filming, and now was paying for the food and drink.

I rode to Hillbrow in the van with the Soweto musicians. Our spirits were high. Celebration was in the air.

At Tangori Chicken we sat at a long table. Kathy Weir hosted, presented the menu, its various options, the various dishes. Her lovely face reflected a glow, one I had grown to need, one that would not be there soon, one I would miss.

Sandele Khemese spoke to me concerning the more serious subject matter.

"See these people at this table? I can tell you truthfully they trust you. But many promises have been made to them, and remain unfulfilled. If you can, indeed, assist us, assist our dreams, you will then find them opening up to you."

140

I expressed the opinion that there was not much time. Lindu and Sandi nodded, agreeing. We drank our beers, ate our choices from the Tangori Chicken menu. Paul and Kathy sat now among us. Paul's always hearty laugh punctuated a comment while Kathy's voice floated above the din of conversation. She continued to graciously meet everyone's needs.

Too soon it was time to say farewell to the Soweto musicians. They had to make the journey back. As I walked with them to the van, they locked arms with me. Lindu and Sandi said to me,

"There is an old expression; We part, to meet."

The van pulled up. I embraced Lindu and Sandi. Suddenly all of the Soweto musicians gathered around me and buried me in their arms with a love that was their way. Africa had cautiously accepted my first steps onto her soil in 1986. I now loved Africa with a joy measurable in her anguish, her despair, and now with these musicians, her love. There was a new voice for Africa's music. These were the parents. I had been blessed to part with their new song for my memory.

I watched them as they drove off. It was the same place in Hillbrow where Kathy Weir had taken me the first night. Hands and faces in the van turned, smiling my way, waving goodbye. Soon they were gone.

I walked with Paul Myburgh to his Mercedes. I was choked with tears.

"Yes, I am also crying, and I will see them soon!" Paul said.

"It is time to feel this. It is time to be full," he reflected.

Back at his house, later that evening, we looked at the film footage. It was truly spectacular. I viewed images that portrayed an event with powerful implications. I thanked Paul.

Later, very late, Kathy made a jug of coffee for the drive back to Pretoria where they would drop me at Reinhold Thaumuller's house. There I would spend my last night sleeping in Africa before my plane flight the next day home.

Once more we lost our way. We found Reinhold's home. It was time to say goodbye. These two had endured my growing. Finally, they both embraced me. Patrick, the stupid American, had won their hearts, as they had always been in mine.

There was a bitter, deep sadness in this parting. Paul embraced me. "Farewell. Go well, my friend. Live long."

I looked into Kathy's eyes. She not only loved me now. She trusted me. "Goodbye, Paddy. We will miss you."

I threw my bag over my shoulder and watched them drive off. Their good wishes became the final, quiet chords of my long journey through Africa.

March 1986, I dreamed of a music from Africa. By May, 1989, Africa taught me to sing and move my body, humbling me to the truth that it must be Africa who teaches us about herself. We, as westerners, have the opportunity to understand by reaching towards Africa's song.

A foolish, stupid American stumbled onto this new day. A disturbing question remains.

Will others from the west embrace this in their heart and their body? Will anyone take this up where it began on that day in Soweto, South Africa? Classical music and the West will gain a new hope for peace with the Soweto musicians surviving and prospering.

The loss is too tragic for me to face.

Lord, make us all instruments of your peace.

EPILOGUE II

This story is finally published. I am still affected by those days in South Africa. I moved to New York City, 1993, in order to live the rest of my life quietly. I compose sonatas in the isolated world of a composer, anonymous among the millions. Writing my South African story disturbs the calm waters. 8000 miles from the Hudson river in South Africa are people who shared with me what has remained my greatest adventure.

Kathy Weir lives in Ireland. A few years back the Soweto String Quartet played there. She was present at the concert. Memories returned and she attempted to contact me at the Fame school here in New York City without success. Prior to this story's publication, I went on a search to find her. Thanks to a kind soul at a film company in South Africa, my inquiry was forwarded to Kathy and we began a long series of e-mails. I wanted to know whether, in her opinion, I had only imagined all we had shared. It was real, she assured me, surprised I had given her such an important role. Her 'Africa' remained with me, I assured her.

Africa remained when I composed music for the October Ballet Company in Ho Chi Minh City, Vietnam, February, 2002. I met them in Bangkok, Thailand when I was pianist for the 1996 Asia tour of the Martha Graham Dance Company. I performed for a week in Bangkok. Tran Van Lai and his dancers had come from Vietnam in order to participate. I met them one morning in the lobby of the hotel where

I was staying, and they greeted me warmly. Would I come one day to Vietnam and compose for them? The question belonged to the days in Africa. I had gone to Africa, I would go to Vietnam.

I visited another people once more because of Africa. This time on the Native American reservations in North and South Dakota. The puppet master pulled his threads once again, November 2001, when I sat next to a United States Probations Officer on a plane. She noticed my New York State driver's license. She told me that she had seen the fire and smoke at the Pentagon from her office window. We had endured the travel inconveniences together from the aftermath of 9/11. She asked what I did in New York, and I told her. Rene Green shared with me special work she spearheaded for youth on the reservations. I asked her whether they had talent. "Do they ever!" she replied. By the time we landed we had mapped out a project eventually named, Share the Fame. The plan was for a school on the reservation to be sistered by my school where dance and music inspired youth to finish school. Hopefully this culturally based curriculum would decrease futility, presently the demise of promising talents among Native American youths. When Rene returned to Washington she called Rich Crawford, chief probations officer in North Dakota. In less then three months from the time I sat next to Rene Green on a plane, we drove from rez to rez, witnessing an overwhelming turnout of dancers, singers, storytellers, and visual artists, all under the age of 20.

The music of the Soweto String Quartet, born in the homelands and developed in Soweto, means that there is the same promise for the cultures of Vietnam and the 'First Peoples'. A noted composer asked me why I felt that the music of Africa needed the West. She felt that African music was complete. I assured her that I was too aware of the quandary. She understood when I explained that it was the musicians in Soweto who embraced this new music's art form. It was a dream owned by Africa.

I have always been, and only been a friend. In Africa, Vietnam, and on the rez , the people received this 'fool' with open minds and hearts.

These dreams are theirs. They desire, deeply, to take their unique place on the world stage, and they are kind and eager to invite us to blend our cultures, as long as we travel towards theirs.

Is there a 'Mozart' in South Africa? Vietnam? The Rez? I believe so. I am a friend to this. The sublime genius sings in every culture. All we have to do is open the mind and become 'fools'.

I tell my African stories to students at the Fame school. They listen, and they believe me, because I first trust them and love them. I am spending these quieter years challenging talented minds and inviting them to become 'fools'. One very gifted student remarked recently, "You are the last of the artists who lives the artist's life, Mr. Byers."

Perhaps. Look to Africa, and then to the East, and when you have done so, look in our American backyard, on the Rez. Watch out for these youths and the ones from the Fame school!

The bliss of Africa is alive and well.

Now, it's your turn.

Some local traditional Native American dancers pose with Reno Green, Washington, D.C., and Patrick Byers, back far left, of New York.

Appendix

Lindumutze MnGoma organized Muse Africa Muse in 1988 in order to create an orchestra from classical musicians living in Soweto, as well as create performance opportunities for the orchestra. The 22 members of MAMS and their mission continues to this day. May of 1992 Mr. MnGoma was invited with MAMS to play for the investiture of Dr. Walter Sisulu at Venda University. Lindumutze MnGoma is a recognized leader for the restoration of the culture in South Africa, a legacy passed to him from his father, the late Dr. K.V. MnGoma of Zululand.

The following list of musicians participate in MAMS and its on going mission.

Vusi MGwena	flutist
Fana Makhaza	flutist
Zion NDlovu	flutist
George Mlangeni	bassoonist
Cyril Khumalo	trumpet
Arthur Mahaltsi	violinist
Patrick Motsa	violinist
Tumelo Motsa	violinist

Benjamin Motsa   violinist
Makhosini   violist
Lindumutze Mngoma   cellist

The Soweto String Quartet came from MAMS. The musicians are:

Sandele Khemese   violin
Thamsanga Khemese   violin
Makhosini   viola
Malusi Khemese   cello

The author filled in for the musical director of Dance Theater of Harlem on a tour in 1994. Members of DTH shared with me the news that the Soweto String Quartet had performed with them in New York City a year before during their regular season. With this news, I was told that the Soweto String Quartet had played at the inauguration of president Nelson Mandela. Their recordings are available at most record stores. Theirs is a favorite of my children, when we camp in the summer, and the car CD player plays music that continues to inspire hope and resurrection.

SEANA MARENA AND MOZART

Writing down the music, Seana Marena, with the tools I work with as a composer, presented unique challenges. This music comes from the body. How can traditional western musical notation get this 'vibe'? I spent an afternoon on the hillside outside the Funda Art Center with Cyril Khumalo discussing this challenge (Boosey and Hawkes often depended on Cyril for assessing manuscripts of African music). We discussed in detail the African triplet and its special musicality, one far removed from the western triplet.

The western triplet is performed best feeling a "two" under the "three". Brahms' music exemplifies this 'feeling'. Debussy was the first western composer to depart from feeling of 'two' under 'three'. His arhythmic phrasing needs elasticity, one with a delicate sensitivity to longer phrasing with a gentle pulse. Cyril told me that he particularly loved Debussy's first movement from A Children's Corner Suite. He said that when he taught this music to the children in Soweto, he asked them whether they believed music could become a butterfly. He played Debussy's music and then remarked,"you see, Debussy has turned this music into a butterfly!"

The African triplet governs the music in Seana Marena. I have written it in common time with triplets. This is a lame presentation.

The triplet quarter. quarter, quarter in eighth notes treats each note with equanimity. The African triplet is closer to dotted eighth, sixteenth, eighth. Even this is weak, because the sixteenth is a "lazy" note, spread in its own space between the dotted eighth and the last eighth of the triplet.

How to write it. Cyril believed that if the music was written in as straightforward a presentation as possible, African classical musicians playing and recording the music could present the 'vibe' of the triplet, while at the same time present accurately other special qualities of the music related to the body.

Jazz is written with standard common time elements. The syncopation is passed from player to player, recording to recording. Hymns and gospel music also fall under this presentation of the musical score.

I wrote down, within my limitations, Seana Marena when I first heard the choir in Shoshanguve. I scribbled 'x's for the feet, for which the choir with their feet, syncopated the music. My feet notation traveled from the township programs with the musicians from the National Symphony, to the unforgettable day in Soweto, when the Pretoria musicians joined me with MAMS to explore this mystery.

Paul Myburgh's film, *Symphony in Soweto*, captured the struggle the Pretoria musicians and I had had trying to play my feet score. The MAMS players patiently explored with us the music's unique phrasing and pulse, and my score's limited presentation. Classical musicians in the United States are always looking at the clock, but the clock was not present those hours at the Funda Art Center. Every musician knew we were in view of the horizon of a new world. The music would have to be developed and owned by MAMS and the Soweto String Quartet, until the musical harbor was built for other ships to port, but it was an exciting beginning.

Paul's film is a beautiful film. Unfortunately, I am not a film maker, and after it aired here in the United States, I did not know what to do with it. It is a timeless film, an historic moment captured, and I hope this book generates interest to give the film a wider audience. Paul took on the entire financial burden making it, and all of us in his film owe him a great debt financially and artistically. Without Paul's film this story would remain one man's written account.

Why Mozart? A classical musician feels music on several planes. A composition is assessed based on technical skill, musical power, the ability to remain fresh and not become dated. There is another plane that is difficult to give words to. There is an essence to certain music that when one musician plays a fresh take on a musical phrase , an appreciative nod from another musician expresses the music's quality. The same notes on a page can come to life differently at times, so much a surprise to the musician, that the execution remains a memory throughout life.

I feel this quality listening to Seana Marena whether sung or played, even with western instruments. The 'shape' of this music is not unlike the 'shape' of Mozart's inexpressibly beautiful melodies.

Listen to the opening bars of Mozart's Menuetto from the 'Jupiter' Symphony. Is there not the same life in Seana Marena?

I hear it. I feel enchanted with the similarity. The soil is the same, the specifics for notation and performance, radically different. This means a potent music is there for the listening and development. We, from the west, cannot write this music unless we reach towards it. Reaching means humbling ourselves.

I 'know' little about African song. I have 'heard' knowledge that resonates understanding of the African song. MAMS and the Soweto String Quartet do not need us. We need them. We need them in a profound way. Africa is where music was born. These rhythms and phrases are our first beginnings.

Our music is lost in a sea of harsh downbeats. Classical music, as well as popular music, pounds us in ordered phrases to keep us alive. We are alive! As Paul Myburgh often said to me, life is long. Only the music of Africa returns a worthy dividend, a life giving, life affirming truth: the sun rises, the day is full, and night gives rest.

An African Mozart coming out of MAMS , the Soweto String Quartet, and other African musicians, humbles me.

I am a friend of this gift from Africa. Whether the reader is now a friend or one day will become a friend, Africa's song, like Africa's people, rises with the sun, lives the day full (even in war and famine), and rests with the night.

It is in Seana Marena. Can you hear it? It is also in Mozart, and I have only begun hearing it since the day in Soweto and Seana Marena.

Seana Marena

Menuetto

"Jupiter" Symphony C major K.-V. 551

W. A. Mozart

SPECIAL THANKS

First and foremost I thank all of the people who are in this book, even Rennie Clarke, the 'bad guy'. When Reinhold Thaumuller and I were ready to add narration to the final edit of African Adagio, Reinhold asked me whether I could let bygones be bygones and invite Rennie to work on the copy. Rennie had a gift so I took Graham Martin's counsel. I shook hands with Rennie. African Adagio included Rennie Clarke's excellent work.

North Carolina Center for Public Broadcasting aired both films thanks to Chancy Kapp and Bill Hannah. Preparing the schedule for broadcast, Chancy confessed to me she was supicious that there was a political side to the African Mozart. She trusted my artistic motives and left politics out of my art. I am thankful.

The following people assisted with the preparation of this book: Lewis Gellman, Martha Beinor, and Jennifer Byers who proof read and checked for continuity. Alison Sawyer, I thank for her faithful friendship in the darkest hours as well as for her assistance helping me with the original journal.

There were and are many american friends of the African Mozart. These include author, John Ehle, actress, Rosemary Harris, the late director, Ellis Rabb, the late North Carolina senator Hamilton Horton, Tom Moore, Katherine Gray, Patsy Gray, Nancy Anne Greenfield, former North Carolina governor, James G. Martin, Ron Sustana, Paul

Brown, Howard Skillington, Larry Alan Smith, Barbara Lister-Sink, Malcom and Johanna Morrison, the Graham Martin family, Lady Faye and the late Sir Leo Arnaud, the Arnaud family and their community of Hamptonville, North Carolina. Paul Green, Nik Munson, Lynn Peters, Dr. John Roach, and a composer's friends of the heart, Betty Anne and Don Linville. Their daughter, Margaret, one of the most hauntingly beautiful girls to grace this planet, died in a car accident months after the filming in Africa. I composed a trio for piano, clarinet, and cello, *A Rainbow for Margaret*, performed at her memorial. Soon afterwards, Don and Betty Anne, yet grieving, visited me. Don drove an 18 wheeler listening to Mozart on his truck's radio. Margaret was a gifted visual artist. They wanted her life to continue via the dream of an African Mozart insisitng I accept monies the insurance company sent them from the accident. I hesitated. "This is what you were born to do, Patrick. Please?" To date, Margaret remains the only composer's muse sheltered by cherubim out of harms way.

Each of these people, like Bettie Anne and Don, had their own reasons for getting involved. When each of them went their own way I was deeply saddened, but I understood. Some have passed away and this saddens me the most, particularly the death of Graham Martin. How does one thank the dead? Graham Martin embraced the African Mozart. He did so with the same zeal with which he served this nation as one of its great ambassadors. Few trusted my instincts as unreservedly as he did. This book stands as a record of his final contribution to diplomacy, albeit through giving time and counsel to a composer of sonatas. (April 2006 New York City)

Seana Marena can be listened to at the website:
Patrick Byers, NewMusicJukeBox
from the **American Music Center.org**

ABOUT THE AUTHOR

Patrick Byers was born in Louisville, Kentucky in 1950. In 1982, the mayor's office of the city of Louisville, and U.S. Congressman, Romano Mazzoli presented him with the key to the city, honoring his work as a native son. He received a Bachelors of Music from the North Carolina School of the Arts in 1972. In 1989 he received a composer's grant from the National Endowment of the Arts for Music for Soweto MAMS (Muse Africa Muse Symphony), a concerto for viola and orchestra. He is founder of Composers Group International, a not-for-profit organization that collaborates in partnership with major arts organizations in New York City for arts in education. He currently is resident composer for the Fame school, LaGuardia Arts High School at Lincoln Center in New York City. He lives in Harlem with his wife, composer Jennifer Byers and their four children, Colin, Zoe, Aubry and Micah.

Printed in the United States
71771LV00004B/267